SOVIET COMBAT DIVERS

in World War II

Pavel Borovikov

Schiffer Publishing Ltd
4880 Lower Valley Road • Atglen, PA 19310

Translated from the Russian by Omicron Language Solutions, LLC.
Originally published as,
"ВОДОЛАЗЫ ВЕЛИКОЙ ОТЕЧЕСТВЕННОЙ,"

Library of Congress Control Number: 2016943575

ISBN: 978-0-7643-5190-7
Printed in China

Published by Schiffer Publishing, Ltd.
4880 Lower Valley Road
Atglen, PA 19310
Phone: (610) 593-1777; Fax: (610) 593-2002
E-mail: Info@schifferbooks.com
Web: www.schifferbooks.com

Contents

Preface

The roles of divers in World War II in Soviet, and later in Russian, historiography has hardly been given any attention, and this is not only wrong but simply unfair as well.

We know about the heroic deeds of sailors, infantrymen, artillery men, tank crews, and aviators, but few remember that diving sabotage and reconnaissance groups, repair and reconstruction and emergency ship-salvage detachments of the Corps of Engineers, the Navy, and the riverine forces moved over the entire thousand-kilometer front, from the Baltic to the Black Sea, together with the armies, along the shores of the seas and of all the great rivers and lakes.

Divers covered the difficult route twice from the banks of the Volga and Neva to the Spree, first side by side with the army in the field, clearing the water routes of mine obstacles, bridge spans blown up, and ships sunk in the waterways, providing for unimpeded fords across rivers and operations supporting the land units of the military riverine flotillas and supply ships, and then when peace came, reconstructing the water routes, railroad and automobile bridges, dikes and dams, river and sea ports, and raising sunken ships.

Hundreds of divers died under enemy fire, from the explosions of bottom mines during mine clearance and from the severe breach of safe operating procedures when diving and surfacing that was forced by the military situation.

The time has come to remember those who have been undeservedly forgotten in the post-war decades, to remember and point out to us today how divers lived in the war, how they fought, and how they died, protecting our homeland.

This book is dedicated to them. Blessed is their memory.

Introduction

In order to present, in a structured fashion, such a multidimensional activity as that of diving operations, it seems appropriate, in addition to grouping diving operations by their types (such as hydraulic-engineering operations, ship salvage, ship repair, etc.), to introduce another subdivision based on the zone in which the operations were carried out, in relation to the front line, even though this subdivision is a conditional one:

- battle formations: in areas of direct contact with the enemy, which were subject to the effect of all types of weapons: small arms, artillery, and aircraft;
- the near-front zone: those areas in which diving units were not in a zone of direct military engagement, i.e. they were deployed outside the direct view of the enemy and were not accessible to small-arms fire, but were affected by artillery fire or bomber aircraft;
- the close rear: areas beyond the reach of small arms or artillery fire but subject to enemy bombing strikes;
- the rear: areas beyond the reach of the enemy.

This subdivision, like any other, is conditional to a certain extent, but it bears a specific and understandable logic in this book's structure.

This book does not consider the formation, merger, and disestablishment of the various diving elements, formations, administrations, and organizations. The book is devoted to diving operations and to the divers themselves, and not to the organizations. It makes no difference to a diver, in general, what kind of "roof" he has over his head; a man is a man, water remains water, pressure is pressure, just as it makes no difference to a bomb what group a diver belongs to or whose head it falls on—the Navy, the Corps of Engineers, the People's Riverine Fleet Commissariat, or the Water Rescue Group OSVOD.

That is precisely why organizational and administrative decisions are accorded minimal attention in this book: no offense meant to anyone who served in the administrative structure.

I will emphasize the sources of information that this book is based on. There are only three types of such sources today.

First of all, of course, there are the documents. No selective, systematic treatment at all of archival documents as applied to diving operations from the prewar and war times to the present. The only reliable, official sources of information actually available on wartime diving there has been operations are the award citations for divers, which have been collected in the archives of the Ministry of Defense and which have become accessible thanks to the Ministry of Defense Internet Project on Heroic Deeds of the People (www.podvignaroda.ru). Analysis of hundreds of award citations has not only enabled a list to be determined, with a rather high degree of reliability, for underwater operations carried out during wartime and the conditions under which they were performed, but it has also enabled us to get a feel for the spirit of the times, to a certain extent, as it is expressed in the words and formulaic phrasing of the citations.

Then there are the recollections of participants in the events, being described, both firsthand and oral narratives. This information is contained mainly in the memoirs themselves of divers who took part in World War II, such as, I.A. Udalov's books *Operation Storm* (Yaroslavl', 1966), and *Tale of the Baltic Commandos* (Moscow, 1968), about a reconnaissance diver in a special-operations company in the recon section at Baltic Fleet Command; A.P. Sobolev's book, *The Madness of the Brave,* on the emergency rescue service in the Northern Fleet (Moscow, Detskaya literatura, 1975); O.I. Tumanov's book about a diver in the emergency rescue service of the *Black Sea Fleet* (Moscow, Izd. DOSAAF, 1978); and a number of similar publications by other authors. The reports of heads of the emergency rescue service have also turned out to be valuable sources of information, summarizing the experience of the organization and the conduct of diving operations in the war years, such as F.I. Krylov's report, "Our Missions," published in the pages of the collection, *Shipbuilding* (Moscow–Leningrad, Izd. Narkomrechflota, 1945). Interviews are of definite interest, especially those held right after the war, particularly if these conversations were with professional divers like V.P. Kozlov, a diving specialist in the Underwater Riverine Unit (Podvodrechstroy).

And finally, a third source of information mainly concerns the equipment used: diving gear, technical means of providing for dives, etc. This source consists of photographs from the war years. They are preserved in state archives and in the collections of various museums, starting with federal government collections and ending with the so-called "rooms to military glory" at military units and in family archives. Unfortunately, photography from the era is rare, yet those images discovered are valuable and interesting, independent of their artistic merit and quality.

Thus, the photos are gathered together in this book are all that could be found in archives or museum collections or on the pages of books, magazines, and newspapers and on the Internet. But this is not simply a rehash. I have not just set down this or that bit of information; I have attempted to analyze, summarize, and evaluate the degree of reliability for the information being presented and to provide a professional assessment of it. Solitary, odd facts gathered in one place (or what the authors of reports present as fact) acquire a new quality in their interrelationship, complementing each other, confirming or refuting this or that piece of information and forming a kind of unified, integrated picture.

There is one more thing I would like to turn your attention to. Very few photographs remain from the war times, as has already been mentioned, which deal specifically with the diving services, particularly from the initial period of the war. This is understandable; the times were extremely tough, it was not a time for photography, and diving operations as such were not especially "photogenic." For these reasons, there are far fewer photographs of divers from the times of World War II than one might wish. To compensate for this, and also to sense a little of the atmosphere in which diving operations were carried out, photographs are included here that were taken in the war years at places where operations were performed, even if there are no divers as such in them.

Of course this book cannot be an exhaustive study; it is just an attempt to systematically treat what is known today about the place and role of combat divers. This is not the end; it is the beginning of the investigation, specifically taking stock of the facts we know, and not just of the facts, but of the legends as well. But all the work, the real research work, from "burrowing" into libraries, archives, and museums to military glory in the military units, elements, and fleets, is an on-going work.

I considers it pleasant duty to express my sincere gratitude for the materials provided and assistance rendered by the Russian State Archives for Photographic and Film Documents, the State Archives for Film, Photographic, and Audio Documents in Saint Petersburg, and the Military History Museum of the Artillery, Engineering, and Communications Forces, and personally to my museum colleague, A.A. Martynov, Colonel (retired), Department Head; to the Museum of the Great Patriotic War, to the Kronstadt Naval Museum and personally to its founder, A. Yu. Mel'nikov, and its archivist, V.N. Shatrov; to I.A. Matyuk, leader of the Belarusian Military Patriotic Club "Poisk" to the State Archives of Volgograd Oblast, the Panorama Museum of the Battle of Stalingrad, the Road of Life Museum in Osinovets, and personally to the museum director, A.B. Voytsekhovskiy, and to Capt. 1st Rank A.V. Kramarenko, D.Tech.Sci.; to Reserve Capt. 1st Rank A.I. Novikov, diving specialist; to Reserve Capt. 2nd Rank A.V. Chumak, diving specialist; to Reserve Capt. 1st Rank E.T. Gadzhiyev; to Reserve Capt. 1st Rank I.I. Gorobets, diving specialist; to diving specialist A.B. Korolev, and many others whose observations were extremely helpful during the work on this book.

I would like to express special thanks to the Dutch expert on diving technology, David Dekker, for affording meaccess to his extensive archive, and specially prepared series of photographs of equipment from his personal museum (David L. Dekker, www.divinghelmet.nl/www.divescrap.com).

Acronyms and Abbreviations

ASG	Emergency Rescue Group
ASO	Emergency Rescue Detachment/Ship-Salvage Detachment
ASU	Emergency Rescue Administration
ASPTR	Emergency Rescue and Underwater Engineering Operations
BMF	Baltic Sea Fleet
DOSAAF	Voluntary Society for the Cooperation of the Army, Air Force, and Navy
ENViR	Unified Standards for Output and Assessment
EPRON	Expedition of Special Purpose Underwater Works
ERS	Emergency Rescue Section
GARF	State Archives of the Russian Federation
GKO	State Defense Committee
GRU	Main Reconnaissance Command
GVRU	State Military Riverine Administration
KBF	Baltic Fleet Command
Narkom/Narkomat	People's Commissariat
NF	Northern Fleet
NKOP	Non-Commercial Enterprise Organization
NKPS	People's Commissariat for Line of Communication

OGPU	Joint State Political Directorate
OSVOD	Societies Aiding in the Development of Water Transport and Saving Lives on the Waterways
OVR	Waterways Guard
OVS	lightweight diving gear
PDP	underwater hole-punch
PDSS	Underwater Sabotage Forces and Resources
Podvodrechstroy	Underwater Riverine Unit
PTR	Underwater Technical Operations
PVO	Air Defense
RASU	Riverine Ship-Salvage Administration
RGAKFD	Russian State Archives for Film and Photographic Documents
RKKA	Workers' and Peasants' Red Army
RO	Recon Detachment
RON	Special-Operations (Specops) Company
SPb	St. Petersburg
TsGAKFFD	Central State Archives for Film, Photographic, and Audio Documents, Saint Petersburg
TsVMM	Central Museum of the Army and Navy
VIMAIViVS	Military History Museum of the Artillery, Engineering, and Communications Forces
VMF	Soviet Navy
VVO	Military Reconstruction Detachment
VVU	Military Reconstruction Administration

Chapter 1

THE PREWAR YEARS

In the middle to the end of the 1930s, the whole Soviet Union lived with a sense of inevitable war, and all its resources were directed toward preparing for it. The heads of the diving services, whether military or civilian, understood that, in the event of inescapable war, the usual problems they solved lay ahead of the divers (emergency rescue and hydraulic-engineering construction), adjusting for things of a specific military nature, to which were also added, of course, purely military tasks, mainly sabotage and reconnaissance actions.

Emergency rescue missions and issues in hydraulic engineering were undertaken and resolved by units of the Office for Expedition of Special Purpose Underwater Works (EPRON), created in 1923 under the aegis of the Joint State Political Directorate (the OGPU), and toward the beginning of the war, within the structure of the People's Commissariat (Narkomat) for Communications, which was practically a monopoly on the area of diving and underwater-engineering operations in the country.

The diving services in the armed forces solved their problems through their own efforts and resources: divers in the navy secured military activities for the ships of the fleet, while divers in the Red Army Corps of Engineers mainly resolved issues on providing crossings over water obstacles and salvaging sunken equipment.

With the appearance, in the second half of the 1930s, of efficient, lightweight diving gear (autonomous oxygen-breathing apparatus with closed-circuit breathing, today called re-breathers) and "dry" suits, yet another diving organization was formed in the prewar country, the OSVOD Union, oriented toward the use of light diving gear. Initially, the tasks of OSVOD divers were water rescues, but in the war, particularly in the beginning, they played their own role, which, surprisingly, was not a minor one, but more on that later.

But over the country there hung the shadow of inevitable war, and preparations for it went on in the prewar years, not only in the army and navy but among the civilian population as well.

The almost paranoid secrecy of the prewar years, warranted to some extent by situations around the country that had taken place at that time, led not only to the citizenry not knowing what the military was doing, not only Army divers not knowing what was being done in the fleet, but the Navy diving services in the fleets (in this case the Pacific Ocean and Black Sea Fleets) not knowing about the light-diver training that the sabotage and reconnaissance groups were conducting. As a result, these organizations duplicated each other in accomplishing the same types of task.

What was the state of the country's diving services in the prewar years?

Fig. 001: Cadets from the EPRON Diving School on tactical military maneuvers, 1931.

The main volume of emergency-rescue and hydraulic-engineering operations was intended to be performed by EPRON forces. Initially, EPRON was a semi-military organization. Its employees wore a military uniform and even went through military training, in addition to diving and general education (Fig. 001), they were on a military allowance, and the entire EPRON, with its people and its equipment, was supposed, in the event of war, to be folded into the structure of the Navy as its specialized emergency rescue service. In a word, that is exactly what happened. In the first days of the war, the EPRON forces were literally poured into the Navy structure, and after the war EPRON was not restored to its former strength, having been broken up into three elements: the emergency rescue service of the Navy; a specialized industrial unit of the Ministry of Shipping, which included basin detachments for emergency rescue and underwater engineering operations (ASPTR); and a specialized industrial unit of the Ministry of Underwater Riverine Units (Podvodrechstroy), carrying out hydraulic-engineering construction and diving operations in inland reservoirs. But that is another story still, and it is not related to the war.

Unlike the Navy, where EPRON was in the Reserves, the Red Army Corps of Engineers, the very ones who made the most use of diving operations in the country's armed forces, could rely only on themselves. The only thing EPRON gave them assistance on was diver training in the beginning of the 1930s (Fig. 002).

Fig. 002: Divers in the Red Army engineering forces, trained at the EPRON Diving School in Balaklava, 1932.

Traditionally, first in the Russian Army and then in the Red Army, the principal burden of arranging fords across rivers and other water obstacles lay with the Corps of Engineers, while the construction and maintenance of flotation means in good repair, including ferry crossings and floating bridges of various types, required the presence of specially trained diving services in the complement of pontoon-bridge units.

It was the task of divers in the Corps of Engineers, in peacetime and in time of war, to search for and salvage flotation means (boats, pontoons, and so on) and various military property and equipment sunk at the crossings, to perform reconnaissance and clearance of the fords, and to provide underwater engineering operations associated with building bridges and laying cable, piping, etc. over river beds and other water obstacles.

According to the *Instructions for Diving in the RKKA Corps of Engineers* (Moscow, Voeynizdat, 1937), dive stations for the engineering forces at the end of the 1930s were equipped with ventilated, twelve-bolt, Siebe-Gorman diving gear. A full set of equipment at a station provided for two divers to work underwater. But in practice, three-bolt Denayrouze equipment was used in parallel with the twelve-bolt Siebe Gorman gear (Fig. 003).

Fig. 003: Preparing for the descent of a pontoon diver in the Red Army engineering forces wearing Denayrouze gear. (Photo from the VIMAIViVS collections, 1930s)

In order to supply air to divers in the dive-station complement, lightweight, two-cylinder, Denayrouze air pumps were included, which provided for operations of normal duration at depths up to sixty-five feet, and with intense pumping, for brief operations to a depth of seventy-eight feet.

Dive station equipment was packed in special boxes and bundles that were easy to carry behind the troops, transported on two team-drawn, double-tree carts (Fig. 004) or, at the end of the 1930s, on a GAZ-AA automobile.

The head of a dive station ran the diving operations in the sapper and engineering units of the RKKA. He was a diving specialist who had had special training and had been certified at the EPRON technical diving school. Nine men made up the complement of a dive station: four senior divers (Red Army members in their second year of service), four divers (Red Army members in their first year of service), and an electrician demolitionist (in charge of a special set of sapping equipment, underwater lighting, and telephone communications).

In addition, all the divers were trained to perform underwater work with manual and pneumatic tools.

The Instructions mentioned above forbade transferring divers from a dive-station complement to other unit elements unless they

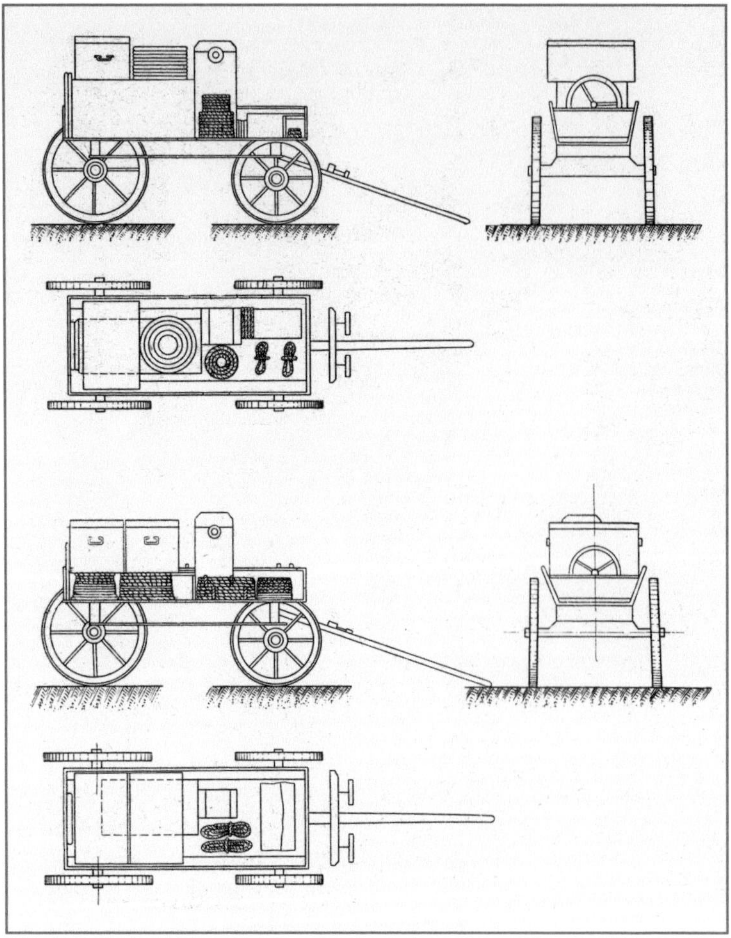

Fig. 004: Placement of equipment from a dive station on two team-drawn, double tree carts. (Instructions for Diving in the RKKA Engineering Forces, Moscow: Voyenizdat, 1937)

did not meet the requirements of the diving specialty. But in the first part of World War II, this stipulation in the Instructions was not observed, and divers in the Corps of Engineers, like other service members in the Corps itself, were utilized not for their ostensive purpose but as infantrymen, which led, in the final analysis, to a severe crisis, provoked by the virtual absence of engineering support for the army in the field in the first years of the war.

Of course, neither was there any question of sabotage and reconnaissance activity, based on overcoming water obstacles in secret, wearing enormous, hosed equipment, although this idea, as the saying goes, was rumored. Only the appearance of lightweight diving equipment based on oxygen-breathing apparatus created the specific preconditions for this.

The first attempt to evaluate the possibility of light divers in a new form of military action, that of sabotage and reconnaissance using diving equipment, was undertaken in the Red Army Corps of Engineers at the beginning of the 1930s. It was just at that time that a group of lightweight-diving instructors was formed in Leningrad at the Leningrad School of Military Engineering and directed to train a group of cadets made up of five men. The training was conducted in the region of the city of Pushkin, on a lake with a specially equipped underwater training range. There is no information on the training program or its duration, but it is known that the program for training recon divers was fully implemented, and a special Commission, led by K.Ye. Voroshilov, head of the USSR People's Defense Commissariat, was at the final training session.

A participant in the training, Mikhail Ostritskiy, recalled this historic episode; he was a cadet at that time, and later, an instructor at the Leningrad School of Military Engineering:

> I was studying at the Leningrad School of Military Engineering when a quota arrived for five students to be selected for special duty. The very healthiest ones were chosen. And I was one of them. They delivered us to Tsarskoye Selo near Leningrad (it was already being called Detskiy then), and they berthed us at Field Marshal Suvorov's former dacha. Some 45–50 of us were accommodated there. The dacha was on a lake. The large lake was Suvorov's. It was deep. With running water. That, they said, is your objective. You will be studying here.
>
> The training began in the fall. The days got cold. The water was even colder. 7–9 degrees ... They began to send us down into the water. The special diving suits, the waterproof dress – all that appeared later. We hadn't even heard about it. They dropped us under the water in an ordinary Army uniform. Summer military blouse. Green trousers. Slippers on our feet instead of soldiers' boots. They also issued us warm underwear; it was warm when it was dry ... Of course, so we wouldn't choke, a clamp on the nose and a rubber mouthpiece, such as amateur underwater swimmers use now. But their oxygen tanks are bigger. Ours were a lot smaller, and had, moreover, an inadequate absorbent for carbon dioxide, which can be the cause of death. Boys lost consciousness in those days.
>
> Everyone who dove was given a weight in his hands so he wouldn't come back up to the surface. They tied on bricks or whatever. When they lowered me down the first time, to two or three meters, it was nothing. When I went down to eight meters,

it was a little scary. Dark. Icy cold; my hands got numb. The water pressed down on me, no joke. My legs cramped up, but you didn't toss away the bricks: you'd be like a cork. You got used to it.

The tasks got complicated. They taught us to walk under water to the other side of the lake. For the purpose of reconnaissance, to seize and hold a bridgehead. They taught us how to hang charges underwater and how to blow up bridges and ships in harbors – that had to be done.

We didn't know that we were the first underwater soldiers in the Red Army; we were just glad that instructors from the Academy of Military Medicine were teaching us, and somehow even Academy member Orbel', a famous man, was there, with lectures on physiology and pathology. We boys had not had a lot of education, but we understood almost everything.

At the end of October, a whole "cavalcade" of light motor vehicles drove up to our "field marshal's lake." We looked and we couldn't believe our eyes: out of the automobiles came Sergey Mironovich Kirov, the highest authority in Leningrad; behind him Voroshilov, the People's Commissar of Defense, and then all sorts of commanders, some with four diamonds on their collar tabs. They formed us up to meet them, the head of the course reported that we were ready to carry out orders, and without any hesitation they lowered us into the water in groups. Each group had its own task: some reconnoitered the shore, others "blew things up."

The weather that day was disgusting. When you went into the water, you noticed: the visiting officers were shivering in the penetrating wind. There were ripples on the lake. But even there, the rain was rattling. And the water too, I must say, was not pleasant ... But it all went smoothly.

Shortly after, the diving instructors announced the Red Army's orders for us. After a time, dive stations for training the troops began to appear in all the military districts. A new and great enterprise had begun, it turned out, and I began to grasp that they were preparing us, not for defense but for offense. Like the paratroops who were being trained not far from us.

In Nikolayev on the Bug River, in Cherkassy and Kiev on the Dnepr, soldiers were being taught to pull light guns over the bottom. At first, it was 45 mm guns. Then bigger ones. And later, any weapon at all. Time wasn't going to wait. The war was going to start any minute, and who didn't know that: the rivers of Europe flow everywhere.

I understood, training at Kiev, what a serious force we were.

There came to us, at the dive station on a channel of the Dnepr in the Vyshgorod region, Army Commander 1st Rank Iona Emmanuilovich Yakir, with a large group of senior command staff. At that time, Yakir was forty-five but he seemed young. Yakir was an erudite man, who spoke about our business as if engrossed.

He laid out the mission very specifically. To go in advance of the attacking troops.

Dry-land divers were widely used in Kiev maneuvers on the Teterev river. We trained the troops, several companies, about a battalion, the first ones in secret; they went into the river before the night fog had dispersed. And when soldiers in underwater gear with two hoses, like aliens from another planet, suddenly rose up out of the water, the border patrol that was guarding the opposite shore at the training areas, simple boys, children really, ran in terror away from the river.

To this day I remember meeting with Yakir at our dive station when he was reviewing out the demonstration training. The commander's joyful face, his excited speech. The review was very detailed. No one forgot Army Commander Yakir.

Our training wasn't easy. It was a time fraught with unhappy incidents. Some sort of group had dragged an anchor along the bottom, with a cable being pulled behind it. When you move under water, the current can carry people off and toss them around. Soldiers were moving behind the cable. But each one of them still had a cord above his head, going up to a float, which moved along with the soldier. If the floats on the water were moving, you knew everything was OK. If a float disappeared, watch out! And then suddenly the floats vanished. It turned out that the anchor cable the troops were moving behind had begun to surface, and the weight attached to it came loose. And the cords from the floats got tangled up in it. The boys tried to surface and couldn't. It was a tragedy; a whole section died, eight men ... They demoted the commander whose men this happened to. This bitter lesson forced us to think again about training techniques and the divers' equipment. There was no greater loss.

In 1936, I was awarded the Order of Lenin for successes in the area of training underwater troops. The Order of Lenin was rarely given then; that was a holiday for all the "dry-land divers." I was only twenty-five. The future seemed unclouded.

After the war, I spent a lot of time and effort explaining how and when to use our method of forcing rivers, which sharply reduces losses in the attacking troops. It turned out that this method wasn't used anywhere. Never. Even though the Dnepr, the Sozh, the Bug, the Prut, the Western Dvina, hundreds of rivers in Russia, Poland, and Germany had to be taken in battle, leaving behind tens of thousands of soldiers at the crossings, dead and drowned. A terrible thing, a crossing under fire. A famous poet, Aleksandr Tvardovskiy, sanctified quite a few places to the crossing in his poem *Vasiliy Terkin*, for good reason, beginning simply and straightforwardly:

"The crossing, the crossing!
A shore on the left, a shore on the right,
The sleet rough, the edge of the ice ...
For whom is there just a memory, for whom glory,
For whom the dark water, –
No sign, not a track ..."

Why wasn't our method ever used? Perhaps there would have been left, among the living, not tens but hundreds of thousands of boys cut down, the ones Tvardovskiy mourned.

I didn't understand that right away. I didn't believe it to be a crime right away ... Stalin killed Kirov, and almost all those outstanding military leaders of the Soviet Union. And Yakir was among them. The new means for waging war that we proposed for reducing losses were thrown away, along with the military leaders who were shot ... And so, meeting a hurricane of fire, soldiers swam, forcing the rivers on boats, floats, and logs.

This wasn't the Second World War but a battle like that with the Tatars on the Nepryadva River or the river Kalka. Who thought about the losses? It's bitter to talk about this. But it was so ...

But all that, it's easy to understood, came later. And then after the first exam at the "field marshal's lake," in the presence of Sergey Mironovich Kirov and People's Commissar Voroshilov, I returned to my own military school to take my exams, quickly "forgetting" about our experience for some reason. I did well in my exams; I was inspired, I would say, and in January of 1933 I graduated. They didn't send me to command a sapper platoon, as had been previously proposed. I began to teach at various "dry-land diver" bases.

There are some very serious moments in these reminiscences, and you'd like them to be developed in more detail.

The absence of equipment was not surprising, in general, for the beginning of the 1930s, although it's not clear what apparatus soldiers wore underwater. Apparently, it was the IPA-1 device, which made its appearance in 1931. And it's not fully understood why bricks were used as weights or why they needed to be carried in the hand and not hung on the belt or simply on ropes over the shoulder.

The attention the senior RKKA command paid to the military possibilities of an "underwater infantry" should be noted. The seniors considered it an independent offensive force similar to paratroops. Ostritskiy pointed out, correctly, it seems, the reasons why this method of conducting military actions was not implemented, but more about that a little later.

Fig. 005: How an RKKA "underwater infantryman" might have looked in the 1930s. An interesting detail of the equipment: goggles with compensating chambers for pressure in the air spaces under the glass as the pressure of the surrounding water increases during a dive.

But what is really surprising, and about which there is still not a word, in any case, in the literature generally available, is the scale of training for underwater troops and the nature of the training conducted. This inadvertently causes reservations. However, it looks as if Ostritskiy deserves to be trusted: in his award citation from 1942, it showed that among his previous awards, he held the Order of Lenin "for successes in the military training of a unit." The Order of Lenin was generally given for something more substantial than simply the military training of a single unit. But it's possible that it was for mastering a new type of military activity. Even more so that it is also consistent with Ostritskiy's own words: "In 1936, I was awarded the Order of Lenin for successes in the field of training underwater soldiers."

In light of what has been said, a totally different kind of story appears on the Internet. "Such units were also in the infantry," his grandfather related, "like the detachment of 'underwater infantry' formed in 1935 from border guards in the Ukraine. They trained them on the Dnepr." This is too much of a coincidence as to time and place with the recollections of Mikhail Ostritskiy presented above.

Information from V.G. Pashits, B.N. Zayakin, and G.V. Malinovskiy must also be regarded very seriously, which we will talk about in the next chapter.

Roughly the same situation as in the army occurred with diving operations in the prewar years in the navy. In spite of the existence of EPRON's affiliation with the navy, the navy had its own diving service, aimed at solving its own, specific fleet problems. The overwhelming volume of underwater operations was carried out using ventilated equipment, both three-and twelve-bolt equipment, manufactured just slightly before the Revolution as well as in the second half of the 1930s and made in EPRON workshops (Fig. 006).

Besides the ventilated equipment, the so-called harbor mask was used in working on the underwater portions of hulls and ship mechanisms on navy ships, in today's parlance light-diving, air-hose equipment (Fig. 007), developed over several years by EPRON engineers in the beginning of the 1930s based on a Japanese prototype, and adopted at the end of the 1930s into the equipment in the navy as shipboard diving equipment. In *Rules for the Diving Service,* published in 1932 and reprinted in 1944, there were even special divisions that regulated how this equipment was used on navy ships.

In the beginning and middle of the 1930s, the navy was equipped with the Series E lifesaving oxygen apparatus developed by EPRON, and somewhat latter with the more refined Series IPA, ISA, and VIA apparatus. Of course, diving specialists in the navy were thinking over the novel possibilities for the military application of light-diving equipment, which was principally new to them, based on closed-circuit, oxygen-breathing devices, which offered considerable time

Fig. 006: Divers in the Black Sea Fleet in review. (Photo: I. Shagin, 1936, from the collections of the Fotosoyuz [Photographic Union] Agency Ltd.)

for operations underwater as a result of their low weight and small size.

The first practical steps were taken in this direction in the navy in the Pacific Ocean Fleet, but this was four years later than the training mentioned earlier for army underwater Spetsnaz [*Translator's note*: special operations or specops]. V.L. Zarembovskiy and Yu. M. Kolesnikov described this in detail in their book *Naval Spetsnaz* (St. Petersburg, 2001). Just a brief description of this training is presented here.

On October 19, 1938, Flag Officer 2nd Rank N.G. Kuznetsov, commanding the Pacific Ocean Fleet, approved a special plan to train a group of light divers: "... based on soldiers exiting from the torpedo tube of a submarine in individual diving gear from a depth of 49–65 feet for the purpose of cutting through an anti-submarine net to force submarine barriers, exchanging sub crews in a submarine underwater, executing a debarkation landing for reconnaissance and to perform an act of sabotage on shore actually using weapons and explosive devices."

Fig. 007: Diver in lightweight diving gear, consisting of a harbor mask built into a TU-1 drysuit.

The training was carried out on October 22–24, in Uliss Bay from on-board the submarine Shch-112 in the presence of members of the Military Council of the Pacific Ocean Fleet.

The following was successfully demonstrated in the training:

- a group of divers crossing Malyy Uliss Bay over the bottom at depths up to seventy-two feet along a cable (they went a distance of 1,312 feet in 15–20 min);
- cutting anti-submarine nets at a depth of forty-nine feet in 10–15 min;
- a group of divers exiting from a submarine underwater and surfacing along a buoy line and another group from the surface entering the submarine;
- debarkation of commandos from a submarine lying on the bottom, through a torpedo tube to shore on a guide line they had set up;
- a debarkation landing under the same conditions along the guide line set up by the commandos;
- blowing up explosive devices and staging a battle using grenades and small arms;

- commandos returning to the submarine on the bottom and coiling up the guide line.

Something similar was also organized in the Black Sea Fleet. In 1940, analogous training was set up and conducted, but on an substantially smaller scale.

The training in the Russian Far East and on the Black Sea was assessed positively, and in 1941, the Navy took the next step: forty men were selected from the personnel complement of the 1st Special Naval-Infantry Brigade, who were passed by a medical committee and began a course of light diver training. In addition, in the process of training, each diver made three exits from a boat through a torpedo tube, a transit with a weapon along a guide line to shore, and a return to the submarine. A submarine in the Pravda [*Truth*] series was assigned specifically for this purpose.

With the beginning of World War II, this trained group of divers entered the complement of a special-operations company, but more about this later.

Thus, at the middle command-level link between the army and navy, the potential for a special-operations and engineering diver unit and the technical possibility of achieving this potential were evaluated as being entirely appropriate and what is more, completely reasonable steps were taken at their level to train these units, including addressing tactical issues in their use.

However, when the new capabilities were demonstrated, everything stopped.

In the 1930s, the country's authorities looked askance at sabotage and reconnaissance activity, seeing sabotage specialists as a potential threat to themselves. For this reason, a network of support bases for the partisan movement was done away with, which had been organized in the prewar years, and the organizers of this network were repressed. Apparently for this very reason, there was no further development or any attempt to create sabotage and reconnaissance groups of light divers in the army or the navy, and they came back to this idea only with the beginning of World War II.

There is one more event in the prewar history of domestic light-diving. The Soviet Navy trained light divers for themselves, to use as shipboard divers. They were all, it may be said, spread among their own ships, and diving was a secondary duty for them, since their fleet specialty, whether machinist, deckhand, or whatever, was of primary importance. Naturally, they were not used as divers at the start of the war, except perhaps to support a ship afloat, if necessary, or for work in a sunken or smoke-filled compartment. The same also applied to members of submarine crews: they went through mandatory light-diver training, but their use as divers on ships other than their own or on other platforms was ruled out.

The EPRON naval diving school at Balaclava also trained light divers, but as a supplement to the principal specialization: working in ventilated equipment.

There is no information in general on the agenda for training light divers in army elements, other than from the recollections of M. Ostritskiy.

Thus, the principal method of executing diving operations in both EPRON and the navy, and in the Corps of Engineers in the RKKA before the war was with ventilated equipment. And, speaking objectively, it turned out that the only element that systematically trained, and used, light divers was the OSVOD Union.

Domestic industry perfected the production of autonomous oxygen-breathing devices at the end of the 1930s, and they quickly drew the heightened interest of OSVOD specialists. Oxygen devices that were lightweight, small, and not complicated to use gained in popularity by virtue of those very properties, both among professional rescue divers, for whom mobility itself was very important, and among amateurs, for whom this was reason enough even then, in the 1930s. Furthermore, this apparatus opened up a path underwater for women as well, and they were fully up to it (Fig. 008).

Created in 1918, on the basis and traditions of the Imperial Russian Society for Water Rescue, which had existed in Russia since 1872, the Union of Societies Aiding in the Development of Water Transport and Saving Lives on the Waterways of the USSR (the OSVOD Union), was founded precisely by virtue of the specific nature of problems associated with saving people from drowning, a natural area for the wide use of oxygen-breathing devices.

And following thereafter, a natural step was that of solving problems in the pre-conscription training of light divers for the army and navy.

In resolving these two issues: saving people in the water and the pre-conscription training of light divers, the OSVOD Union had already, by the middle 1930s, created a series of diving schools within its own structure and had begun to turn out dozens, if not hundreds, of civilian light-divers.

V. Kronshtadtskiy, founder of the first light-diving school in the OSVOD system, its instructor and a fixture there for decades, wrote in 1940:

Fig. 008: Female light-diver in the OSVOD Union. At the beginning of World War II, such women replaced the men who went to the front and acted as both light-diving instructors and divers at the Stalingrad crossings. (Photo from the RGAKFD collections)

After 1938, light diving in the USSR began to grow extremely rapidly. The station, in the course of one year, introduced light diving into the riverine and maritime fleets, into the riverine police, into the fishing industries, and into mines for rescue work in flooded sections.

A total of 142 light-diving stations were active in bottom-clearing operations on the Narcomrechflot line, where the productive labor of the light divers significantly raised the work standards of heavy divers. Naval vessels deploying into the Arctic also began to be fitted out with light-diving equipment in order to resolve ship breakdowns at sea.

At biological research stations, in survey work when building ports, and in other operations, the sealed diving apparatus won a firm place for itself. At OSVOD, light diving became a leading form of life-saving technique. Nowadays, not a thousand light divers still stand watch in the rescue service. Thanks to this new type of diving technique, dozens of people have already been saved from depths that were previously considered "lethal." Light divers from OSVOD saved several ships and mitigated dozens of cases of accident damage at hydraulic-engineering facilities.

Fig. 009: Student practice dive, OSVOD light-diving cadets, end of the 1930s. (Photo from the RGAFKD film collection)

> Light diving entered into the life of the country as a full-fledged form of diving technique.
>
> OSVOD, where light diving was beginning to have great applicability, received permission from the government to independently train light divers and the command complement of a light-diving service.
>
> In 1936, OSVOD made the first attempts at light-diving operations in sealed apparatus, and in over a total of three years, a thousand light divers were already working underwater. Not a single capitalist country has achieved such rapid growth in diving cadres and techniques. Such growth could only occur in a socialist state where, under the wise leadership of the great Stalin, free people passionately create a happy and joyous life.

V. Kronshtadtskiy's evaluation of light diving as such and its place in the country's economy sounds rather substantial, although with the inescapable adjustments for the rhetoric of the prewar years.

Indeed, after several years, divers were an essential part of the complement of OSVOD rescue stations. For instance, the

Central Rescue Station in the city of Astrakhan had in its complement three divers, three dive signalmen (it is not very well understood who these were, but apparently they were ones we now call support divers), and a medical worker. Aside from the Central Station, there were two more rescue stations in the Astrakhan region, also with divers on their staff.

And there were dozens of such units in the OSVOD Union throughout all of Russia. Thus, by introducing divers into the regional staffs, having their own diving courses, and publishing professional literature independently (Fig. 010), OSVOD actually created a full-scale specialized diving structure, paralleling the diving structure of the People's Communications Commissariat (NKPS), represented by EPRON but independent of it.

The expediency of a similar approach to forming a reserve of divers was corroborated all the more with the beginning of World War II, when OSVOD, in parallel with the diving courses of the Soviet Navy, was nearly the principal source of light divers for the front and in the rear, but there's more detail on this in the next chapter.

Furthermore, up until the war, light diving attracted not only young men but young women as well, for whom the low weight of the breathing apparatus made it fully accessible for use. And it was precisely these young women who replaced the men who went off to the front at the start of the war, who were diving instructors and on-the-spot light divers working underwater, both at OSVOD rescue stations and in the close rear of the army in the field.

It was in just such a state that Soviet divers approached the beginning of World War II.

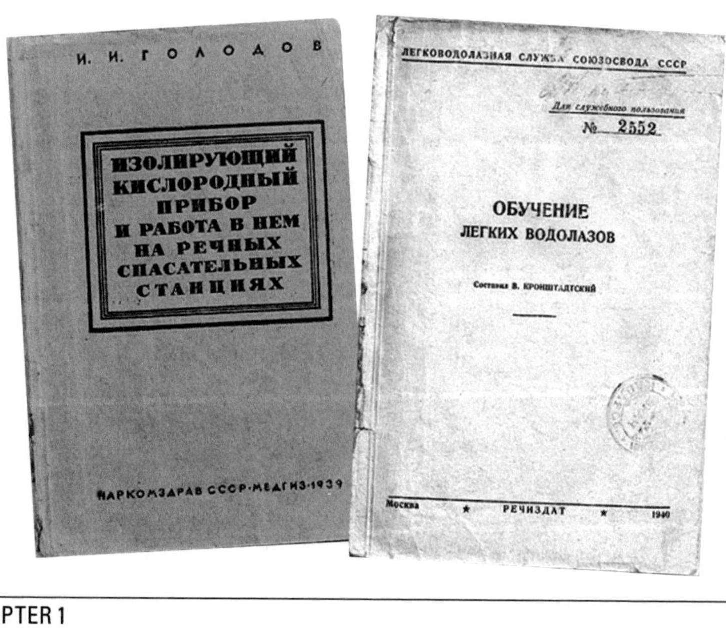

Fig. 010: Professional diving books, published in the OSVOD system in the prewar years.

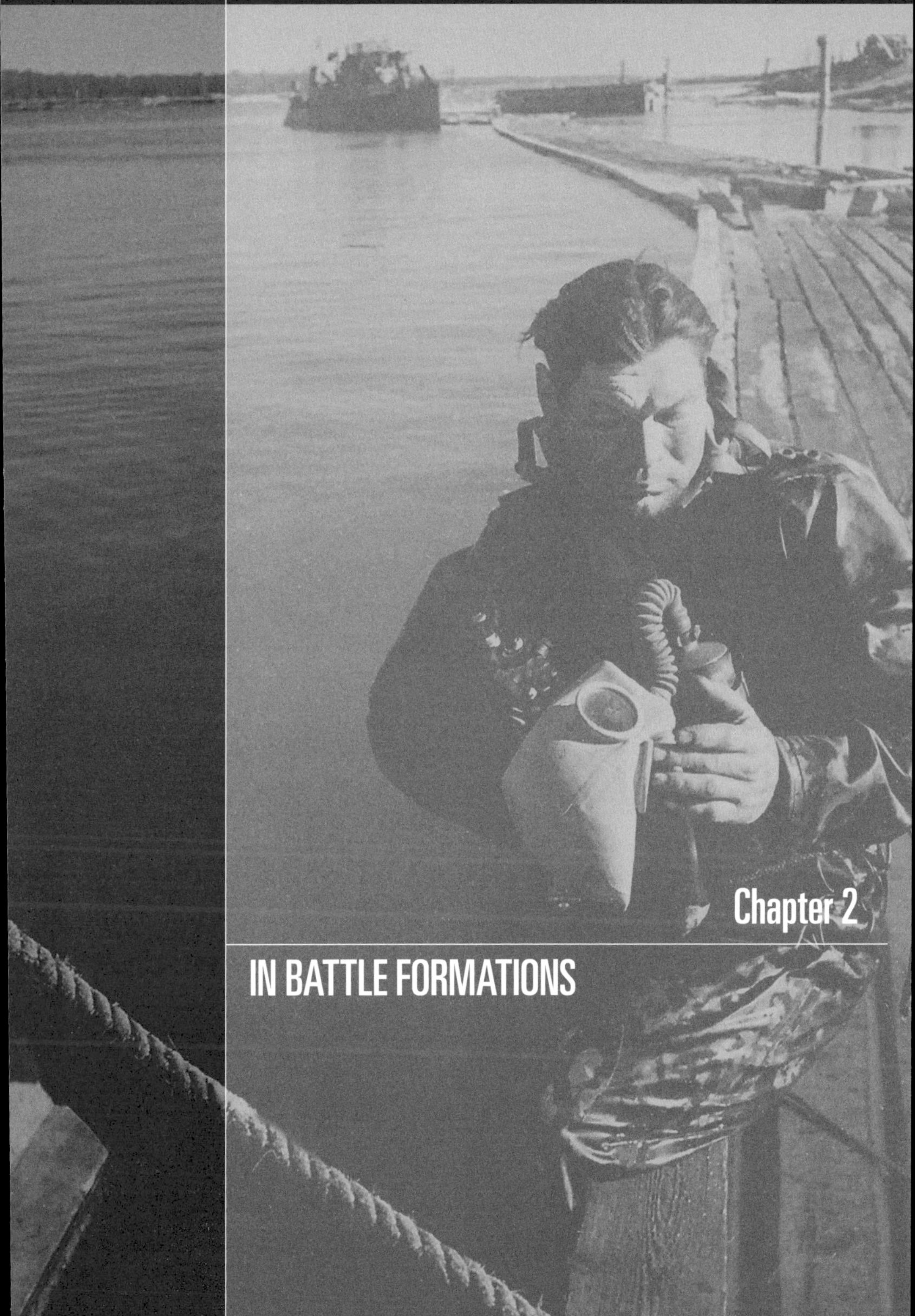

Chapter 2

IN BATTLE FORMATIONS

During the war, only a few divers in sabotage and reconnaissance groups took a direct part in military actions, and later, a lot of rumors of such cases spread around, of varying reliability. Let's try to sort out what the truth is about these rumors, what is dubious, and what is frankly fantasy.

Let's say right away: the only special unit verified by documentation is the special-operations company in the reconnaissance section of the Red Banner Baltic Fleet command, I.V. Prokhvatilov's company. All the rest are unconfirmed, as the recollections of participants in World War II are not confirmed by documentation or are related "secondhand."

The First Days of the War

We have already said that diving in general, and light diving in particular, was quite well developed before the war in the Soviet Union, and it developed along three lines: the navy (including the militarized EPRON), the engineering branches of the Red Army, and the OSVOD Union. The army and navy, naturally, were ready in earnest for the use of divers as military units. Those and others, as was seen earlier, conducted appropriate training; they came close to creating suitable units and even began forming them up here and there, but—they did not succeed in this.

With the start of the war, the navy, and the army, addressed this issue.

A specialized sabotage and reconnaissance unit, a special-operations company or, as it is usually called, a RON, was created within the structure of Soviet Navy in August 1941. Almost simultaneously with the formation of the RON in the navy, attempts began in army elements to form their own analogous diver sabotage and recon units.

V.G. Pashits, without question a professionally literate man, wrote in his book *The Underwater Spetsnaz of Russia* (Moscow, 2006), that in August 1941, a decision was made by the USSR People's Defense Commissariat, to assemble, five miles from the city of Gorkiy in the small town Mokhovyye Gory on the shores of the Volga, a group consisting of twelve light-diving instructors who had graduated in 1940 from the All-Union Central Command Staff Courses of the USSR, OSVOD Rescue Service. The purpose of the assembly was to train the personnel complement of a specially assigned rifle regiment for forcing water boundaries in an underwater variant. In his book, he even presents a photograph of the instructors in this group (Fig. 011).

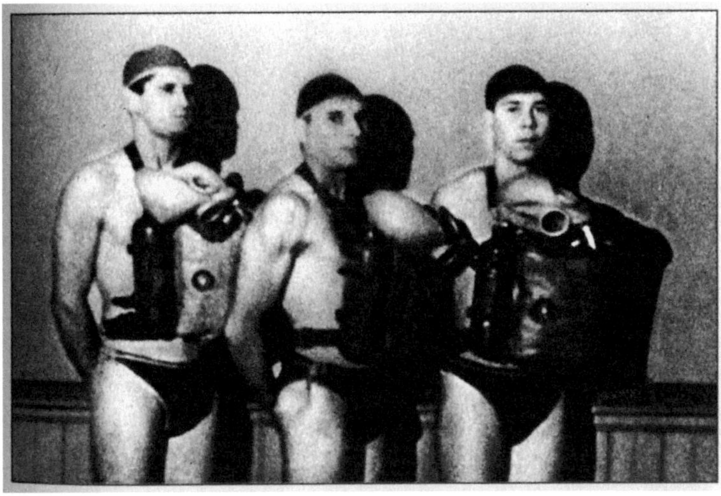

Fig. 011: Light-diving instructors who, according to information from V.G. Pashits, conducted the Gorkiy light-diving training of troops in an infantry regiment, turning them into "underwater infantry." (Photo from V.G. Pashits, *The Underwater Spetsnaz of Russia.* Moscow, 2006.)

Training of the command component was conducted in the initial stage, and then the commanders of the platoons, companies, and battalions taught Red Army soldiers while the instructors monitored the training. The training program was calculated to last a period of a month and a half. Type VIA-1 and VIA-2 breathing apparatus was used (close-circuit diving gear), consisting, at that time, of OSVOD rescue equipment. Metal chains were used as weights, fastened on fire hoses and worn on the shoulders (under the arms), as well as cast-iron weight belts. Later, there came in to the unit the IPA-3 equipment (a close-circuit underwater apparatus), and suits (separate jackets and trousers).

The theory course was flat-out brief; the main emphasis was on practical operations. As the initial dives underwater were completed, the training elements become complicated. Emergency situations were introduced and the soldiers then entered training in walking underwater with the sections in a cluster (Fig. 012). Hermetically sealed magnetic compasses were used as bearing indicators, with a knob for ease of use. It seems that in Gorkiy they attempted to "resuscitate" the experiment that had been drawn up by the prewar army diving service and which was described in the previous chapter.

However, nothing is known about the subsequent fate of this unusual unit.

B.N. Zayakin writes in his own book about something similar: "In the first half of October 1941, the training of an underwater dive group began, numbering fifty men, whose commander was Lieutenant Kreyman. After completing its training, the complement was transferred to Stalingrad, where it provided for equipment and troops to ford the Volga."

Fig. 012: An "underwater infantry" section in training. It might have looked like this during World War II. The time and location of the shot are not known, but this photograph was taken either during the war or immediately afterward. In any case, the divers' gear and their weapons correspond to what the Soviet Union had for equipment at the beginning of the war.

Once again, there is no information on the details of using this group for its true purpose. And, in a broad sense, might it be that both Pashits and Zayakin were writing about the same group?

B.V. Davydov found some interesting information in a collection of documents on the Voronezh Front (category: operational division 2843, case 77, Report of July 20 to September 15, 1942 of Headquarters 6A on the Conduct of the Petropavlovsk, Korotoyaksk, and Storozhevoye Operations). In this document, on page 33, the following is mentioned: "A half-company of divers (37 men) crossed as a fast-strike group to the western shore of the Don, destroyed a military outpost of the enemy, numbering as much as a reinforced platoon ... three of the enemy were killed and seven wounded."

This fact, we believe, which is well confirmed by documentation, fits nicely in the general line of attempts to create light-diving sabotage and recon units within the army structure.

What is more, other independent confirmations also exist of the use of saboteur divers by Soviet forces to destroy enemy river crossings, in particular across the Don. In an award citation for V.K. Gushchin, a diver in the 130th Detachment of the emergency rescue service of the Black Sea Fleet, the following was stated: "Senior Red-Navy sailor Gushchin has been serving in the fleet since January 1942. In November 1942, Gushchin was in a platoon of sixty-two Army divers, where he demonstrated daring and decisiveness in executing military missions for Army Headquarters by blowing up German fords across the River Don. In the direction of Kotel'nikov, eight crossings were blown up, for which he has the thanks of the commander of the Stalingrad Front."

An award citation is an official document, and therefore it is something to think about here, especially in view of Mikhail Ostritskiy's recollections described in the previous chapter, who was an instructor at the Leningrad Military Engineering School.

And, to finish with the stories of attempts to form special diver units in the RKKA, here is one told by an expert, G.V. Malinovskiy, a historian on the Corps of Engineers, in the book *Brigades of the Red-Army Corps of Engineers, 1941–1945* (Moscow, 2005. pp. 24). He wrote that it was proposed in 1943 by the Corps of Engineers to form a brigade of "watermen," who would become a reserve for the Main Supreme Command. The brigade was to be composed of a brigade command (forty men), a company command (120 men), and seven battalions of "watermen" (each with 520 light divers equipped with IPA-3 close-circuit underwater apparatus); a total of 3,800 men in the brigade.

The brigade was intended for reconnoitering water boundaries, destroying enemy crossings, capturing bridgeheads on the opposite shore, setting up obstacles in enemy territory, and laying and clearing mines at fords, as well as for sabotage at the enemy rear, providing underwater work when constructing and rebuilding bridges, convoying military cargo underwater, and conducting emergency salvage operations underwater.

But there is no more information about this element anywhere. So, was this what was described earlier: yet another attempt to resuscitate the prewar projects for training an RKKA underwater Spetsnaz?

Thus it can be established that attempts to create specialized sabotage-recon units in the armed forces of the Soviet Union during World War II were repeatedly initiated, but only the sailors in the siege of Leningrad executed them, who formed the specops company already mentioned, better known as the RON, in the recon section of Red Banner Baltic Fleet Command, under the command of Senior Lt. I.V. Prokhvatilov.

A Special-Operations Company

So much has been written about the specops company in the recon section of KBF Command that we do not intend to repeat it here. But in order to complete the picture, let's pay a little attention to it all the same, although only briefly.

It was created in August of 1941. In the company complement were cadets in the EPRON Vyborg diving courses and forty men selected at the beginning of 1941 from the complement of the 1st Special Naval-Infantry Brigade and from those who had already gone to Oranienbaum before the war for special light-diving and sabotage-recon training. Senior Red Navy sailor Ivan Udalov, an RON soldier, recalls in his book *A Tale of Baltic Commandos* (Moscow, 1968), written down just after the war:

> Competitions were arranged in speed of movement and endurance. Several men entered the water at the same time at the pier and went by compass in the direction of the island of Vol'nyy. The norm was to go some four hundred meters in twenty minutes. Sevka Anan'yevyy invariably held the record: a light-haired fellow, always smiling, a young man from Leningrad. He got to the island in seventeen or eighteen minutes.
>
> I got there in nineteen, taking a different route. The ground was muddy there; if you stood for a few seconds to catch your breath, suddenly there was an impenetrable cloud of murk. You couldn't see the luminescent compass arrow, and one diver, losing his bearings and finally getting confused, had to come up to the surface. When the kids got into the clear layers of water and managed to reach the goal, Nikitin and the old "Capt 2nd," who was invariably present at the training range, gloated. They considered that one of their tasks was to instill stubbornness, perseverance, and boldness in us.
>
> It was especially hard for all of us to exit from the torpedo tube of a submarine and to return. The operation resembled going through the eye of a needle. Well, that was where you would sweat! As your undershirt was wringing, the steam poured off your head when you took off your mask.
>
> A torpedo tube is a metal tube about half a meter in diameter and up to six meters long, polished inside to a mirror-like shine. You had to go into it with your diving apparatus on your chest, your weights, and the reel for the field-phone cable between your legs. They shove you into the tube, and farther along, you know. You can't push off from it, because everything's all slippery. You have to crawl three or four meters, and then the hatch just slams shut behind you, the muzzle door opens up ahead, and the water comes in. Hands on your stomach legs stretched out, you're on your right side. And then, pushing off with your fingers, you begin to bend like a worm: you're stretched out, you're compressed, and you're moved forward centimeter by centimeter. On the boat, everyone is just sick and tired of waiting, and you're still puffing. But look, there's the water! Right away it gets easier. You tie the end of the cable to the boat and, unwinding the reel, you go off in the assigned direction. After completing the mission, you return the same way. The boat is still lying on the bottom. They're waiting

> for you. They pump air into the torpedo tube to blow out the water. Hold on more strongly, or else they'll spit you out like they spit out the torpedoes. And there's nothing to hold on to at all.
>
> Exiting from a torpedo tube isn't for everyone. Some men are eliminated, going to supplement Petty Officer Lukin's detail [*Author*: the administrative unit].

In a maximum approximation of combat conditions, even though they're our guys, who aren't expecting an attack or soldiers, the problem of capturing an "identification prisoner" was also worked out. I.A. Udalov writes:

> They trained for operations at night. They exited from a boat underwater onto the beach, they tracked down a guard who was nodding off and, not letting him collect himself, they stuffed a gag into his mouth, bound his hands, dragged him unceremoniously to the water, and only there did they release his gag, put a mask and oxygen apparatus on by force, and then hauled him, on a rope like an obstinate sheep, into the water. The one chosen for this role was selected fairly by lot. Everyone took turns being an experimental "identification prisoner" for twenty-four hours, and after that he had a rest. But it couldn't be any other way.

The numbers in the company changed periodically, but roughly they stayed at about 130–140 men.

The best known operations of the company: providing work on fords across the River Neva in the region of Nevskaya Dubrovka (RON soldiers, operating both as commandos and as divers, under constant enemy fire, raised military equipment and ammunition from under the water), operations along the route of the Road of Life on Lake Ladoga (surveying the route in the winter of 1941–1942 and later, raising sunken cargo from motor vehicles and barges), blowing up the mooring at Peterhof (November 1942), boats at Strelna (October 1943), discovering stations for aiming FAU-1 aircraft shells on the lands of the Pishmash Factory in Leningrad, searching for and finding the German U-250 with the latest torpedoes with acoustic self-guiding warheads on-board and extracting, even before raising the submarine, secret documents from its compartments (July 1944; more detail later about this operation), providing a commando landing on Rukhnu island and taking part in clearing the island of Germans besieged in the woods after the island's capture (December 1944), and a whole series of others, more than 200 operations in all, and almost half of them using diving gear.

I.V. Prokhvatilov and his soldiers from KBF Command were awarded decorations and medals for these operations.

The first RON soldiers had already made an appearance in August of 1941, blowing up the bridge across the Narva River. At night, two commandos floated with the current, the senior of whom was Senior Lt. Pupkov (the last name of the second one has not been preserved in the archival materials), towing a naval mine with a timed fuse to the bridge, fastened it to a footing, and returned safely home. The bridge was destroyed when the mine exploded.

From a diver's point of view, one of the most complicated missions was blowing up the wharf at Peterhof. It was decided to use two divers to set two naval mines, Model 1908/39, under the wharf and explode them. Naval mines usually consist of a spherical, floating military casing about three feet in diameter and weighing 600 pounds, stuffed with 242 pounds of explosive and connected to a steel mine-mooring cable with a heavy anchor trolley weighing more than 660 pounds (Fig. 013). Apparently, in order to use divers, the mine casings were detached from the anchor trolleys and the horn fuses taken off. Additional ballast was hung on the mine casing so the mines' buoyancy was close to neutral, and the divers could pull them behind by cable loops attached to the casings. For sapping, additional fuses with a timer were hung on the mines. The mines went out with the divers round the clock, just so the divers could learn how to move around underwater with all that.

For the mission, they went at night on an armored gunboat, towing a dinghy behind them with the mines. At the Peterhof dam, they anchored and dropped the mines overboard, and three divers and four rowers boarded the dinghy. Taking the mines in tow, the dinghy silently left for Peterhof. At a distance of barely 1,312 feet from the wharf, the divers dropped overboard. All three of them submerged. Korol'kov, the group commander, got his bearing for moving by compass, and with a telephone cable to unwind, as they moved along, from a reel hung on his gear, he ensured the cable was attached to the bow of the dinghy to show the way to return. Behind Korol'kov, holding onto the phone line stretched out behind them, divers Spiridonov and Zventsov towed the mines. Only a diver could fully describe what it was like for them: in complete darkness, walking along the bottom, with an oxygen apparatus on their chest, whose rubber breathing bag could be torn if they were hit, either drowning a diver or else ensuring the diver would suffer barotrauma to the lungs, towing massive mines after them, travelling hundreds of meters and then having to find the moorage, place the mines underneath it, and not be detected. Ivan Udalov remembers:

Fig. 013: Naval anchor mine, Model 1908-39. Prokhvatilov's men used only the military mine casing: a steel sphere with 242 pounds of explosives, after the horn fuses had been removed.

The dinghy went without a sound. No guard, no wharf, no other shore observation post, no one could have suspected.

When the dinghy had approached so close to shore that it was possible to distinguish the outlines of objects, they turned to port. The rowers left the oars in the water and the dinghy stood still. A couple of hundred meters to go to the wharf. They carefully dropped anchor.

Korol'kov measured the depth—eight meters and a little more—just like it said on the chart. To start with, they submerged the mines, after letting the required amount of water into them. Korol'kov dropped down onto the bottom along the mooring cable, then Spiridonov, and last Zventsov.

The cable of the field-phone reel had been set at the dinghy bow to a length of half a kilometer. The commandos had to return along the cable underwater, back to the dinghy.

On the bottom, they tied themselves together so they wouldn't get lost. Korol'kov had an underwater compass, lined up on the wharf. He took the cable in his left hand. Spiridonov and Zventsov each pulled a mine behind them. They went along smoothly, without catching on the bottom or bobbing upward.

They travelled for thirty minutes, and they hadn't reached any pilings yet. They had obviously missed their aim, going off course somewhere. Korol'kov stopped, they came to a standstill and Spiridonov and Zventsov bumped into one another.

The darkness was absolute. Only the compass face was glowing. The commandos couldn't see one another; they could only make themselves understood using pre-arranged signals, tugging on a thin connecting line. The signals had been worked out for just such a situation. A hand on the shoulder meant stand still. One tug – go forward, two – go right, three – go left, four quick ones – turn back, a bunch of quick, hard tugs – cut the line and surface.

Korol'kov put his hand on Spiridonov's shoulder, and then on Zventzov's. But still, what to do? It's possible to walk in darkness as long as there's oxygen in the tanks. Someone had to go up to take a new bearing. It was Korol'kov's decision, and he made it.

Feeling around, he found the right hand of one of the men (he had already determined by then that it was Spiridonov's), handed the guide cable from the dinghy over to him, which was shy about ten meters which was enough for him to get to the surface. Then he let air into his oxygen bag and slowly broke away from the bottom. Spiridonov and Zventsov stood as if dug in. The least little movement might have tangled up all those linking, guiding, and towing lines, and all would be lost. Often on the training range, operations broke down because of some irregularity on the part of one of the commandos, when everything had been worked out to the smallest detail.

But that was in training, and now they had to summon all their strength and self-control. They were right under the enemy's nose, and the timer on the magnetic mine, that had already been started on the dinghy, was counting off the seconds. And even though they had had plenty of time to spare, they had walked off, one after the other.

Floating to the surface, Korol'kov couldn't immediately believe his eyes: the wharf was literally two steps away. They had simply not reached it yet. Letting the extra air out of his breathing bag, he dropped to the bottom and gave the signal to move forward.

Korol'kov calculated when they would find themselves under the wharf, among the pilings, and now he was walking with his left hand stretched out in front, turning first left and then right.

And there was the first piling, slippery, as if coated with grease, and behind it the second, and the third. They were driven in all in a row, as pilings are.

The commandos pulled the mines farther under the wharf. Spiridonov tied his to one of the pilings. Zventsov took off his Magnitka and attached it to his mine. With his hands, Korol'kov felt the work of his helpers, was satisfied, and touched first one and then the other behind the diving apparatus on their chest. That meant the operation was over and they could go back.

In the dinghy, they had already been waiting for the commandos for a long time. As the cable from the reel was still unwound, at first they snubbed it down. But then it began to wind up little by little, pulling those who were down below all on its own. And there, all three of them floated up to the surface.

They helped them back into the dinghy; they took off their diving dress and weights. All three were silent, breathing heavily and wiping their sweaty foreheads.

But Prokhvatilov himself was waiting for the saboteurs on the armored gunboat. After midnight, when the time allotted for their return had passed, he ordered anchor to be raised to go look for his men. And then: "We had just raised anchor when suddenly out of the water a tower of light rose up. A blinding light, as if self-generated. A double explosion struck our ears. It lifted the boat up, so that I almost flew overboard." The gunboat found the bruised Korol'kov and the oarsmen and collected them from the water; they had been thrown out of the dinghy, which had overturned. Spiridonov and Zventsov had vanished. All the rest of the night, the gunboat hunted at Peterhof, searching for the fallen divers, but with the dawn, it fell under fire and departed.

The divers were found. The air in their breathing bags had kept them afloat, but the wind had carried them off to their own shores. They picked up one of Prokhvatilov's men at the shore battery; the second one had been tossed out onto the shore and left, exhausted, right in the surf zone.

Based on the recollections of RON soldiers, one other operation could be reconstructed that was typical for divers in the company: our commandos tracking into the enemy rear. The details of these operations have been scattered in various places, but for purposes of clarity, they are collected below in a certain operational sequence. In this case, the task to be executed was to insert two commandos into the enemy's rear:

In Bati ... his plan was to throw two commandos, whom he had brought with him, across the forward lines. While still in Luga, we had quickly taught them to how to manage the light-diving gear.

We tested our equipment one more time: the diving dress and apparatus, the security of the weapons' packing, the rations, and the area maps. Only the senior man, Volodya Borisov, had an underwater compass. We tied ourselves together with a strong cord so as not to get lost under the water.

At first the bottom was solid, and it was easy to walk. Then our feet began to get stuck in the mud. We hadn't gone more than halfway when we began to feel no bottom at all under our feet. We could only move forward by floating, holding to the depth specified because of the oxygen in the breathing bag of the diving apparatus. It wouldn't have been hard for one man to go the distance under such conditions, but there were three of us all at once, tied together; it was an extremely complicated matter.

The mud near us was so turbid that Borisov stopped to look at the compass needle. Darkness was all around, although our eyes tingled. It was useless to go any further: we had lost our bearing. Borisov gave a command to cut the cord we were tied by and to surface.

It was as if the Finns had been waiting for us. Just as our heads emerged from the water, machine guns immediately started firing. We had to drop down again to the bottom.

Under water, you couldn't go any further in the impenetrable darkness. And you couldn't see how to turn around and head in the opposite direction. We surfaced several times to orient ourselves, but in spite of the Finns, it just had to be done. Now they were already watching for us. Nevertheless, we gained our own island safely. Night fell, like a gift.

The next night, we went off toward the left, closer to the cove. The water there was in constant motion, and hopefully there wouldn't be large deposits of mud on the bottom. Our guess was confirmed, and we forced the water boundary without any particular trouble.

We spent the whole day on a little island, well camouflaged in the sand underneath bushes. A house was the only structure there.

On the third night, going under the water in the same manner, we found ourselves at a larger island. There were more Finns there; they were walking about freely, up and down. We hid ourselves in the rocks (there were a lot them in the water).

It wasn't the pleasantest thing to lie the whole day right under the barrel of a machinegun. The water pressed down on you, like sin, on the lower parts of your body, and you had to be exceptionally patient to wait for dark, when you could stand up and take off your diving dress, if only for a few seconds. It's hard to imagine any moment happier than that.

The slope where Hitler's pals were was fortified with wire obstructions. We had to cross through them.

Right away, we began to study the terrain, the enemy's movements in the trenches, the disposition of emplacements. We went in two groups: Frolov, along with Gupalovyy and Sinchakovyy, "made noise," to draw attention in case we got hung up, and we guys—Spiridonov, Zventsov, and me—after resurfacing half a meter upstream, led the commandos. A marshy lowland began on this side of the river, almost from the very edge of the shore, changing further on into alder woods, overgrown with nettles, raspberry bushes, Spiraea, and God knows what else.

Through the woods, and then across the lowland, flowed a small stream toward the Narva. Our commandos would penetrate along it to the rear. We had to make a passageway for them through barbed wire that was stretched in several lines across the channel mouth.

A complicated matter, to cut the wire underwater. In a diver's mask, it always jingles in your ears, and it seems that you still hear something or other. One good thing: no mines in the water, and it was a convenient depth at the mouth; they couldn't see you from a few meters away. Misha Zventsov was working with the cutters, and Spiridonov and I silently pulled the ends to one side and fastened them behind the supports so they wouldn't jiggle. There, one line was ready, then a second one, and the third ...

The commandos are lying on the sand, their masks off; they're saving their oxygen, which they'll need when they steal through into the rear along the stream bottom. They wait. One has a German officer's uniform under his diving dress, another has a soldier's. He's accompanying the officer. He's carrying his "bag," and in the bag, wrapped up in a waterproof cloth, a little bit of rations to eat.

There, the passageway is ready. Above the water, the supports look like supports, the wire like a wire, but you can slide through underneath. The boys set off.

And this is just an example of the individual diving operations of soldiers in the specops company; there were more than a hundred of them.

In those days, industry did not play around with special gear for divers, and especially not for the diver-commandos. For work under water, the RON soldiers (Fig. 014) used VIA-2 type oxygen-breathing apparatus, with a reserve of oxygen in a tank, which allowed the diver to transit a distance of up to 2,296–2,624 feet over the bottom. The E

Fig. 014: Reconnaissance diver from a specops company, Recon Section, KBF Command.

and TU-1 drysuits protected the divers from the cold water, with boots stuck on for walking along the bottom (there were no flippers then); they found their bearings using magnetic aviation compasses and reels with a cord to lay out the return route. To conduct military actions on shore, RON divers used an ordinary rifle (before firing on the surface, the bolt had to be opened, and the barrel lifted up for the water to pour out of the bore; you could fire after that). RON soldiers made a lot of their own equipment themselves, which is supported by documentation, in addition to the recollections of the RON soldiers. In the archives of the Ministry of Defense, an award citation is preserved for: "... a light diver in Specops Company, Recon Section, KBF Command, senior sailor Mikhail Il'ich GROMOV ..." for the medal "For Military Service." It stated on the award citation: "From the spring of 1942 on, GROMOV labored in the workshop that provided apparatus and equipment for light commando divers, making dinghys, inflatable jackets, and suits. For providing well for recon operation applications, I request that GROMOV be awarded the Military Service Medal."

But in the intervals between battles, the RON divers did not sit around with no duties. In an award citation: "... to the group commander of Recon Detachment, Specops Company, KBF Command, Master Chief Petty Officer Aleksandr Nikolayevich KOROL'KOV for the Order of the Red Banner." It stated: "In addition to executing military recon operations, Comrade Korol'kov, as a diving specialist in navigation, rendered great assistance in 1943 to OVR boats by replacing screws and repairing underwater damage, for which he more than once received the thanks of the boat command." It is remarkable, but in the collections of the Museum of the Great Patriotic War, the photograph of A.N. Korol'kov shows him acting in this very capacity (Fig. 015).

The RON operated as a part of Recon Section, Red Banner Baltic Fleet Command, up until the end of the war and was disestablished in 1945 due, in the opinion of Fleet Command, to the "lack" of the need for such a unit.

To round out the history of the RON, a couple more considerations must be added, although this goes, to some extent, beyond the scope of this book.

First, the creation of the RON was a completely successful measure, although limited in general application, and the RON experience was utilized over several years in the creation of units of combat swimmers in the Soviet Navy.

And secondly, based on the nature of the operations executed, on the number of them and their results, and on the equipment being used, Specops Company, Recon Section, KBF Command was fully comparable, and in certain respects surpassed, the so-called "K Command," the command of German combat swimmers who operated under similar conditions in the territories adjacent to the Baltic Sea and who had a similar mission, namely that of swimmers, in the same way that super-small submarines and manned torpedoes in the German variant are somewhat related to diving. But, as usual, much has been written with admiration in our country about "K Command," but to date, there has been no full-scale study giving an account of our RON in ordinary literary language, which would be interesting not only to a group of extremely respected specialists, no doubt, but to the average adult as well, thinking about how it was to live at that time, in that world.

However, getting back to our subject, we point out that, in addition to the descriptions of RON military actions confirmed by documentation, there are, based on the pages of memoir literature and on the Internet, rather a lot of stories "bruited about" regarding divers who in one way or another took part in wartime in sabotage and recon activity. And although the authors of these tales are sometimes well known and the

Fig. 015: A.N. Korol'kov, RON recon diver, during the repair of an OVR boat. (Photo S.G. Shimanskiy, May 1945, from the collections of the Museum of the Great Patriotic War)

details of their stories are entirely consistent with the times being described and the specific nature of the equipment used, there is no definite link to time or place in them, and it's sometimes impossible to check those stories. And where they can be checked, they're not always verified.

Nevertheless, these stories are interesting in and of themselves and, being collected in one place, they create a certain picture.

Military Diving Yarns

Let's begin with the story told by K.D. Zolotovskiy in his extremely interesting book *Underwater Masters* (Leningrad, Detgiz, 1958). Zolotovskiy himself, an EPRON diver with many years of experience, was working at the time of the Leningrad blockade in that very city, on the Road of Life on Ladoga, and it appears that he participated in some manner in RON operations. The people mentioned in this tale, such as Boris Kindinov, an EPRON diver, were also well-known personalities. In his "diving tales" written for children, Zolotovskiy describes a number of events, known from other sources as well, such as blowing up the wharf at Strelna along with the boats based there, various commando operations, and a number of others. In these tales, he is quite accurate, and there is, in principle, no basis for not believing him and his story about a skirmish under water with German sapper-divers, although from the point of view of a diver, it sounds, to put it mildly, amusing.

The following is his tale in a somewhat abbreviated form:

> Aerial reconnaissance first noticed a suspicious flurry of activity by the Germans at the hydroelectric station [probably on the Svir river, although this is precisely a case in which the storyteller indicates neither the place nor the time of the event being described – *Author*]. It was reported that a dinghy regularly approached from the enemy shore toward the hydrostation tower, it would stand there for half an hour and go away again.
>
> It was decided to find out what was going on.
>
> A diver, directed to reconnoiter in his light-diving gear and a demagnetized oxygen tank for his breathing apparatus, reported that there were no mines below the power-station tower, but at the base of the tower, boxes had been set down with TNT in them, and the diver brought one of them back with him.
>
> It became clear that Hitler's guys actually intended to blow up the hydrostation tower, just as they had blown up the dam earlier, and the only thing left to do before the explosion was to assemble the electrical wires with a fuse. But this could be done with just a few divers.
>
> Five divers in ventilated equipment were sent to confiscate the explosives and intercept the German sappers. The current where they were working was strong, the bottom firm, with coarse-grained sand; a slippery yellow clay was encountered in places.
>
> The water was clear enough: with a light, everything was visible all around for a distance of two and a half meters, and

farther on, the bottom and the water blended into a uniform yellowish fog.

Petty Officer Podshivalov, as the most experienced diver, approached the tower first, carefully bent down, and dug out a box with TNT, but at that instant the Germans appeared, also in ventilated gear.

A clash under the water was imminent. Here everything depended not just on the bravery but on the experience of the divers as well, since the current was very strong.

The enemy divers, seeing us, stopped. We stood there too. The only thing heard were the bubbles burbling in the valve and the air hissing in your helmet.

You can't get any momentum underwater; movements are slowed, it's not like fighting on land. And if you take a hard swing with your knife, it doesn't land where it's supposed to.

Podshivalov leaned eagerly toward me and said:

"Go left, downstream, take the enemy by the signal line and hose! Grab the hose, you know, seize the diver by the throat."

Nikitushkin quickly caught up one of the hoses and held on to his German by force. Then the German slipped on a rock, he was dragged downstream, and he found himself with our divers. They caught hold of him there. But while our guys were tying the German up by the hands and feet with his own signal line, since he had been knocked out, several of Hitler's pals were already advancing on Podshivalov, who had gone off toward the tower wall to give battle under its cover.

Boris Kindinov rushed to the Podshivalov's aid. He grabbed one of the enemy by the shoulders and knocked him down onto the bottom. But one of Hitler's pals arrived in time from the side and hit Boris's light with a stone. All at once, sprays of glass went everywhere, and they drew a web pattern right across Boris's face, and bubbles seethed out of a hole. Kindinov's suit deflated; it collapsed on itself as if the diver had suddenly lost weight. But considering what he had to do, he quickly tilted his helmet, covered the smashed opening with his palm and called for more air. Farther off and some time before, I had been keeping track of the battle. I stole upstream as far as possible so the enemy divers wouldn't grab my hose. There I found on the bottom the dark branch of a stump that was invisible in the sand and dropped my hose behind it. Then I took it in my hands by its rings, as a fallback, and rushed downstream. Enemy hoses and signal lines were beginning to come my way at some distance from one another. I found first one, then two more.

Three hoses were in my hands. A fourth diver bled off his hose downstream not far from me.

I quickly cut off the enemy's hemp signal lines and thin telephone wires with my knife, and I twisted the hoses tightly with a piece of lacing that hung on my copper weight ring. Nikitushkin, with Kindinov's assistance, hooked those hoses behind a boulder that was projecting out of the sand, and the two of them turned the boulder over with a strong jerk and pressed the tied hoses down.

Now the Germans were swinging on them, like fish drying on a cord.

I hurried toward Podshivalov to help him best his enemy, but suddenly I sensed that I had run out of air. I turned around quickly. A couple of meters behind me stood a German diver, bending over; he had cut my hose and was already breaking it up to the spiral wire, placing the hose on his knee. He was a sixth German, one we hadn't noticed before. It was all becoming horrible and strange for me in my silenced helmet.

I took two unsteady steps toward the German, gathered as much of my strength as possible, and struck him in the side with my knife near his lead weight. He fell and started rolling in the current.

Then I grabbed my severed hose from the bottom and broke it off myself. Now I only had to just casually touch my head to the sliding valve in order to save the last drop of air remaining in my suit. It should be enough for about four minutes. I ducked down and picked up the woven string from my lead clodhoppers, first one and then the other, with my knife. The boots immediately fell off my feet. Now I could be loosely flipped head down and carried off by the current, but I quickly straightened up. Now, off with the weights! I cut off the braces that connected them to my shoulders.

I was torn forcefully off the bottom and carried upward. On the way I tipped upside down twice and bobbed up to the surface, all puffed up like a bubble, swaying in the middle by the cord: this cut into the signal line. And they brought me to shore, like thread on a spool, by the signal line. On the ground, I still managed to hold onto the alarm signal.

When they took my helmet off, I thought that the air had never been lovelier than it was on our shore. Miraculously, it smelled of pines.

By then, they reported that Nikitushkin, Kindinov, and a third young diver had already returned and were carrying loads.

Only Podshivalov was still at the tower. He had needed a second signal cable from the shore and he quickly ordered us to drag it back.

We quickly detached the cord. A German appeared out of the water in a brass helmet with the stump of a hose. Podshivalov came out of the water fast with the boxes of explosives. Trotting behind him, Nikitushkin and the young diver carried rolls of electrical wire and a bunch of fuses. Kindinov came out of the water last. He was protecting his smashed light with his left hand, and with his right he was lugging up from the bottom three copper enemy helmets, burnished by sand under the water and connected to the signal cord.

The following story was told about Black-Sea Fleet divers by Viktor Sokolov in *Neptune* magazine (2002, No.2, pp.53–58):

In 1942, during dive training at Novorossiysk, aerial reconnaissance revealed that the enemy had gone to sea in boats and self-propelled barges and was conducting underwater operations there. Furthermore, the pilots saw divers going down, and there were no bubbles on the water's surface at the dive site. That meant that the Germans were working in gear with closed-circuit breathing, so-called rebreathers. It was suspected that the Germans were mining possible routes to disrupt an assault landing at Tsemes Bay, Novorossiysk. An "identification prisoner" was needed, and it became clear where to get hold of him and what gear he would have.

The submarine Shchuka [*Pickerel*] was directed to carry out the mission with a group of experienced divers.

The transit from Tuapse to Novorossiysk went without a hitch, and by nighttime the Shchuka had risen to periscope depth not far from the entrance to the port. Looking over the sea, the divers were sure that the entrance to the inner waters of Tsemes Bay, a seaport staked off from the sea by thick breakwaters, had booms that they opened with a tugboat in front of each vessel entering port. They decided to send out a commando to verify more accurately just what the German barriers were. The boat surfaced at night, and a couple of divers headed out, swimming toward the booms. At that time, our divers didn't have rubber flippers. Instead, they wore "goose feet" on their boots—that's what they called the webbed fins made to resemble the feet of a goose. There were no compensators or diver delivery vessels then either. They made shift with improvised means, a car inner tube to assist in staying afloat while swimming on the surface. Each of the divers had an ISA-M breathing apparatus, knives, and small lanterns.

The recon was successful, but the result was disappointing: they discovered the entrance to the port was blocked by a strong boom with antisubmarine nets made of steel rings, hung with nests of small antiship bombs. They decided to penetrate into the bay by following behind an enemy ship. So they waited for one.

Entering port behind a regular ship that they cleared the booms for, the sub swung around and settled on the bottom. Now the divers had to get started.

They allotted two men for the underwater operation, the most experienced ones, Pavlov and Korolev, and rigged them for the season and the task set. On top of everything else, Pavlov, who would go into the water first, held a reel of wire, sort of like Ariadne's thread. When all the preparations had been made, Pavlov climbed into the torpedo tube. Groping with his right hand for the knob of the bypass valve that supplied oxygen from a tank, and with his left squeezing a ring for sending signals, he slid in, pushing the reel with the guide thread in front of him.

The steel torpedo tube was liberally smeared with grease so a torpedo could fly out of it easily. The grease also helped the diver: his gear didn't snag, and his shoulders, although straining, slid through. But the darkness and the sultry air were unbelievable.

Steaming like after a sauna, everything smeared with grease, the diver slipped out, finally, from the torpedo tube. Freedom! Getting his wind a little, Pavlov tapped out the signal: "Exited OK." The operation, which was expected to take a total of two hours, had begun.

First thing, Pavlov attached the end of the guide wire behind the overhang projecting from the sub and hung the reel on his back. Then, finding his bearings by compass, he moved forward. It was not hard to go over the sandy bottom, he jumped over small stones, but his feet sank into muddy patches on the bottom, and he had to swim breaststroke above them. And there, beginning to show up, was the dark side of a sunken cargo ship. Somewhere ahead greenish shadows were wiggling, like ghosts. Pavlov was getting a little closer, sliding along the side of the ship in order to stay invisible against its background. He sat down and began to look around. Already now, he could clearly discern enemy divers in green Draeger wetsuits with reddish-purple cuffs. Looking through the murky fog, Pavlov noticed a barge too, next to the cargo ship. And enemy divers were working on it as well. They evidently wanted to turn the sunken ships into a huge mine field, to blow it up when our torpedo boats and landing craft started to break through into port. And the Fascists were preparing such bottom booby-trap mines, to all appearances, a lot of them.

Ten minutes passed before he could distinguish, from among the German divers, two who were wearing trophy Soviet ISA-Ms. One of them was not carrying or packing up anything himself but was only giving conventional signals. Just as if he were the Germans' head guy. The target was established, and Pavlov was trying to decide how to approach him. But the German solved the problem himself. Seeing a cloud of murk appearing unexpectedly, he turned toward Pavlov. Pavlov, half-concealed by the "smoky curtain," beckoned the German toward him. Then the German, apparently thinking that something had happened to one of his people, came closer. And thereupon Pavlov threw himself on the German. Staggering back, the German pulled out his knife. Protecting himself with his left hand from the knife raised up to swing, Pavlov seized the German by the mask with his right hand and hit the back of his head against the iron side of the cargo ship. The German rolled over, dropped his knife, and went limp. The mouthpiece fell out of his mouth, and air bubbles boiled out of it; the breathing bag of his apparatus immediately "got thinner." Pavlov, without hesitating, tucked the German's mouthpiece into place, snatched out his knife, cut through the German's signal line, and tied it to a piece of metal, smiling to himself: "Now let them ask the piece of metal how their commander is doing."

Then he grabbed the German under the arm and carried him off, as light as a feather. The German was in a half-swooning state, which let him be carried like a ragdoll, but nearing the boat, he suddenly regained consciousness. Fritz understood at once where they were taking him, and he tried to resist; he didn't at all want to slide into a torpedo tube, whose muzzle door was open. He had to knock him senseless again, hitting him hard on the back of the head on the Shchuka's overhang. Then Korolev slid into the tube legs first and pulled the senseless German after him by the apparatus straps, and Pavlov hustled in behind him. When all three were in the tube, Pavlov tapped out the assigned signal. The door slammed quickly shut, the boat began to rise from the bottom.

For all three to slide through the torpedo tube was even more difficult than for just one. All three of them were stuck in the tube, and only when they let the water pour out of the tube and opened it could our comrades grab Korolev by the legs and little by little pull all three into the boat. Luckily, at the very same time, the

Germans opened the boom, letting their own ship out of the bay, and the Shchuka slid happily out of the bay behind it.

Everything is pretty much correct in these notes, too. Both the details of the gear and the description of the exit from the submarine through the torpedo tube, as well as the specifics of a hand-to-hand underwater skirmish in light-diving gear, but the problem with this is that nowhere else is there a word about the operation. And there ought to be some mention of it. True, this is, first of all, a unique event in itself. And secondly, the event occurred during training for an assault landing at Novorossiysk and simply not much was written at the time about this landing or the Malaya Zemlya bridgehead they seized as a result, while a lot, except for that "wonderful" fact of the capture of a German diver, might not have happened at all. In any event, we should know about this story, but... everyone is silent about it, even such people who are knowledgeable about the diving history of the Black-Sea Fleet as V.G. Yurganov.

How is it related to this history? On the one hand, it may be some sort of "yarn," but on the other hand ... It is known that in the complement of the Baltic Fleet spec-ops company already mentioned, there were divers who went through training to exit from a submarine lying on the bottom and return to it through a torpedo tube. It is also known that sometimes those divers were called away to a command for some time and then returned, and of course without explaining the reasons why. So perhaps this was one of those "command performances"?

An extremely esteemed man, I.V. Merenov, the author of many books on diving, describes just such a case too:

> In 1944, the battle was already raging in the cis-Baltic, but numerous islands still remained in German hands.
>
> A pontoon bridge had been built across a narrow strait, over which you could only move at night, since it was shelled by enemy artillery from a neighboring island. But the point is, the pontoons were damaged almost daily by the shelling and they sank. The problem was entrusted to a group of divers under the command of Petty Officer G. Sokulin, to raise the bridge and patch up the damage. And so it was on that very day that diver V. Krotov went down for a look at the sunken pontoons. Dropping to the bottom and looking around, he noticed another diver was walking along behind a pontoon, dragging some sort of object. "Where did he come from? I came down alone!," thought Krotov. And it suddenly dawned on him: "A saboteur!" Krotov signaled for an emergency lift; he was brought up immediately and he reported to the petty

officer. What should he do? How could he capture the saboteur? He was armed, of course, and he had special gear. They quickly made a decision: drop three men down, one after the other, right at the pontoon. And that's what they did. First Krotov went: he lay down on the pontoon and began to look around.

The saboteur was standing on the bottom and fastening something to the pontoon. When divers Khudyakov and Stupnev had also descended to the pontoon, Krotov pointed out the saboteur to them. There was no telephone connection. From the surface, the divers had communications along a signal line, but they could only indicate by handsigns to one another. And it was complicated by the fact that the regenerator apparatus the divers had descended with had rubber breathing bags, located on the divers' chests. It was easy to puncture the bags, and to even bump it was risky for the diver.

The capture plan for the saboteur was conceived in an instant: one diver would stay at the pontoons and the others would go around the enemy from two sides. And that's what they did. Khudyakov and Stupnev sank to the bottom, while Krotov, in order to draw the attention of the saboteur, began to scratch on the pontoons with his knife. The plan was a success: the saboteur stopped his work and began to climb onto the pontoon to find out the reason for the sounds he heard but didn't understand. At that instant, Khudyakov and Stupnev threw themselves on him and grabbed his hands. Krotov lent a hand from above. The scuffle didn't last long; they brought the saboteur up. Interrogated, he told about the charge set and the way to disarm it. The bridge was saved.

Yet another story has been travelling from magazine to magazine. In it, a classic sabotage operation is described about divers deep in the enemy rear. This story is written down based on the words of a participant in the sabotage, since the staff members of the magazine in which it was first published (the author of the article was Viktor Sokolov, in *Neptune*, 2001, No.3, pp.56-62) met with the author personally. However, no archival or any other type of confirmation has yet been found:

1943. Preparation was going on for the battle at Kursk. The Germans were concentrating their forces toward the front line, actively using the railroad bridge across the Dnepr River. The command had posed the problem of blowing up the bridge, but mine fields, barriers, and emplacements surrounded it. All attempts by the partisans to overcome the obstacles and approach the bridge had failed. Our aircraft could not bomb the bridge: numerous antiaircraft batteries were positioned around it. Only one way remained to get access to the bridge: underwater.

The operation was carefully planned. It was decided to create a special sabotage detachment, including experienced, volunteer light-divers. Training proceeded under the leadership of Vyacheslav Ivanovich Kronshtadtskiy-Karev, a legendary diving instructor, first at the training ground and then at Podmoskov'ye, at the bridge across the Oka river in the Kashira region. Both the bridge and the river were similar to the Dnepr: the Oka was wide there, up to 984 feet; the current was fast, half a meter per second, almost the same as in the Dnepr, and the waterway depths were also similar, from 10–16 feet.

In the course of the training, Viktor Khokhlov, a professional diver from the prewar period, turned out to be the best. The group's complement included, besides him, a radioman, a doctor, a sapper, a sniper, and machinegunners. They had all graduated from the same program: swimming and taking bearings underwater, firing Soviet and German weapons, engaging in hand-to-hand combat, parachuting, going on multi-kilometer marches with a load, camouflage, running around in the woods without a fire or hot food. A group of commandos was also selected, who had learned German in their spare time, which should provide additional cover.

The gear was chosen with particular care. It was decided to use the durable and reliable TU-1 drysuits adopted as equipment in 1939 and the well-recommended closed-circuit ISA-M oxygen-breathing apparatus, considered to be the best autonomous domestic apparatus (Fig. 016). The underwater route for a diver was not expected to be short, it was hard to estimate the submerged time needed, and for that reason, aiming to increase the time a diver could remain underwater, special attention was paid in training to replacing the main oxygen tank underwater, when it was depleted, with a auxiliary one. This operation was practiced in nighttime dives and was reduced to an automatic action.

The method of the clandestine delivery of explosives to the bridge was a complicated question. At first, they tested the charges hung on an inflated automobile inner tube, but it turned out that the load was impossible to stabilize at the specified depth: it either bobbed up to the surface or it sank. In the end, they decided to use the cork inserts from lifejackets. The boxes of explosives, drifting with the current, had to be slowed down in time at the pilings and fastened to the bottom, and this was another problem.

Fig. 016: Light diver in gear similar to that worn by Viktor Khokhlov to blow up the bridge across the Dnepr River in 1943. (Photo from the collections of the Museum of the Red Banner Baltic Fleet, city of Baltiysk)

They considered several ways to blow up the charges and they settled on electrical fuses. An electrical explosion backed up by a special mine fitted with a timer.

When everything was ready, the group with the full set of equipment flew out to the assigned region. They parachuted in the dark, but everyone landed safely. They quickly buried their parachutes, gathered in a group, and moved off toward the river. Besides their equipment, which consisted of four to five spare oxygen tanks and cartridges with chemical absorbent for the carbon dioxide that would form while breathing, each one carried one of the boxes with TNT. The entire load could not be transported at one time, so they had to make another trip the next night. All together, they carried some 1,102 pounds of explosives.

Fig. 017: Viktor Khokhlov might have looked like this when blowing up the bridge across the Dnepr River. The diver is wearing a TU-1 drysuit with boots for walking on the bottom and an oxygen-breathing apparatus on the chest. The photograph was taken soon after the end of the war, but the equipment for a light diver remained the same as at the beginning of the war.

They chose a place for camp in dense bushes, some seven-hundred meters from the bridge, behind a small promontory. It was dangerous to come any closer; the guards might notice. The commandos were concerned about clearing any mines at the approach for a convenient drop to the water, hidden from the enemy. They didn't make a fire, they just ate dry chow; they didn't smoke. Very carefully they reconnoitered the approaches to the bridge. They discovered that, roughly 492 feet away, the Germans had posted a guard, which consisted of two boats and a cable with buoys stretched across the river.

They chose a moonlit night for the first sally. Viktor Khokhlov went into the river with his oxygen equipment, pushing a reel in front of him with the field wire. He had to lay the wire to a bridge piling. For camouflage purposes, he was wearing meshwork on his head made of twigs, in case he had to surface. There were boots on his feet and a weighted belt, extra heavy in order to tackle the current around the bridge pilings more easily (Fig. 017).

The closer Khokhlov moved toward the waterway, the faster the current ran, and at the waterway itself, its rate reached a meter a second, while the depth exceeded five meters. Luckily, the diver found the bottom sandy and not muddy. Sometimes stumps had fallen down, which stuck out from the bottom, and Khokhlov had to carry the reel around them.

He particularly wound the wire around one especially large stump in order to fasten it down. Now a diver would not risk losing his way back. He could see so well that even the weak moonlight penetrating down to the bottom was enough for him to distinguish individual objects. There was just a little wire left on the reel, and Khokhlov guessed the bridge shouldn't be far away. He also sensed this from the changing nature of the current.

Suddenly, he was pressing up against a solid surface. He instinctively stretched his hand out, groped for a piling, and latched onto it. Rummaging around with his hands, the diver knew that the "wall" was the side of a cargo truck. He quickly guessed that some sort of automobile lay alongside the bridge, probably one of our "ton-and-a halfs," submerged with crates on board. Several crates lay on the bottom.

Khokhlov carefully fastened the guide wire to the truck. He could go back now.

He slid back along the bottom against the current on all fours, holding onto the wire. The struggle against the current took a lot of strength, and, reaching the stump the wire was fastened behind, Khokhlov sat down to take a breather. There he felt that he was having difficulty breathing. He tried to increase the supply of oxygen using the manual trigger, but he couldn't do it. *"Time to change tanks,"* Viktor thought. "What luck, that it happened right here and not under the bridge."

Switching tanks, he continued moving along the wire. In about twenty minutes, the depth began to lessen, and he carefully stood up. The water was chest height. Khokhlov heard the assigned signal: a duck quacking. Moving his legs with some difficulty, he went directly toward shore. They were waiting for him.

The next night, no less hard a task lay ahead: to reach the pilings and set two boxes of explosives underneath. They provided an assistant diver to help Khokhlov. They used the wire laid down earlier to the bridge as a travel line, buckling their carabiners to it with leads whose ends they had fastened to their belts. Khokhlov went first, his comrade behind him. Each one was dragging a box with TNT, to which were tied cork floats to make them lighter.

The divers got to the bridge with no particular problem and, cutting off the floats, they let the boxes with the explosives sink down, and they fastened them onto the piling itself. Now Khokhlov decided to check what was lying in the crates that had fallen off the truck, and he broke one of them open. They turned out to be cartridges.

The divers took a little breather and moved back along the wire on the way back. They slid along on all fours, holding onto the cord for safety. Khokhlov, moving around the stump first, suddenly felt a big jerk. The safety cord on his belt had tightened, and Khokhlov knew: something had happened. He pulled his comrade toward him by the safety line: he was unconscious. Heaving with all his strength, Khokhlov dragged him to shore, which luckily was right there. He pulled the injured man out of the water, ripped open his suit with his knife, and freed him from his gear. His comrade's head was splattered with blood and he was barely breathing.

It was still a ways to the camp. Khokhlov took off his gear, buried both sets of gear in the shrubs near the shore, and loading the injured man onto his shoulders, took off for the camp. From time to time, he gave the assigned signal, the quacking duck. Soon he heard an answer: a "duck" quacking from the bushes.

The injured man had had a concussion; in all likelihood, he had been struck by a floating log. Examining the patient, the doctor said that his life was not in danger.

Nevertheless, the detachment commander decided that now Khokhlov would have to operate alone. In any case, there was only one professional sapper-diver left to spare.

For four nights in a row, Viktor labored at the bridge, making two trips at night. In the morning, he simply fell down from exhaustion, but he finished his job. Ten boxes with TNT were placed under the bridge piling and under the truck with the shells, alongside the piling.

The last trip was the most crucial one. Khokhlov set the electrical detonators, connected a wire to them, and hung a back-up mine with a timer on the boxes with the explosives, which was set to operate in twenty-four hours. "If the electrical explosion fails, the mine will go off," the diver thought.

After finishing the preparations for the explosion, he returned, once again along the wire, to his mates. The next day, he went off for a rest and to eliminate all traces of the group having been there. At the same time, the commandos watched the bridge, waiting for a train to appear with tanks. A train arrived toward evening, and when the steam engine got to the end of the bridge, they blew the bridge up.

After the explosion, the detachment left for a partisan base in the woods, from which they flew out by aircraft to the Podmoskov'ye base.

Later, it was revealed from German military archives that the enemy attributed the explosion of the bridge to aircraft. The Germans couldn't even conceive of Soviet underwater saboteurs.

The main hero of this story is Viktor Khokhlov, a well-known personality, whose military biography included, moreover, serving in Stalin's guard during the Tehran Conference of "Big Three" Allied leaders. But of this operation, the sapping of the bridge across the Dnepr, no additional data could be found from other historians.

There is one more curious nuance to this story. In the same magazine, *Neptune*, but a year later (2002, No. 2), Anatoliy Mukhanov wrote about his meeting with Viktor Khokhlov and he presented the following in Khokhlov's words:

> At night, we, along with the commander, reached the Lubyanka in a passenger car sent to receive Gen. P.A. Sudoplatov ... Based on the sort of interest and attention we met with, we understood that demonstrating the capabilities of underwater swimmers in the basin had finally resolved all the doubts the leadership had had. Then the general declared that the High Command was placing great hopes on creating such detachments, which would be free to make unexpected strikes against the enemy from underneath the water, and it considered that this new type of weapon deserved a broad introduction partisan combat practice.

This information is consistent with materials found by the journalist S. Aslezov in the archives of the Central Committee of the Communist Party of Belarus in the beginning of the 1970s while preparing his book *People of Legend* about the Byelorussian partisans.

The essence of the information Aslezov found is as follows. After one of the unsuccessful attempts to blow up a bridge across a river using a raft, floating with the river current, with explosives and a contact fuse, which was undertaken by the Plamya [*Flame*] Partisan Brigade operating in the Pukhovichi region of Minsk Oblast, the idea was born at the brigade command of blowing up bridges from under the water, using light divers. There apparently were soldiers in the brigade complement who had received light-diver training before the war in units of the Red Army. In any case, in the brigade documents, it was mentioned in this regard that they had mastered the method of conducting combat actions. "This method of fighting against Fascism should be applied in the most active form," it said in a report prepared by the brigade staff for the Central and Byelorussian Headquarters of the partisan movement. The head of the brigade staff, Maksim Filippovich Tarikov, prepared the report on this matter, whom Aslezov met in 1973.

The "underwater warfare" project developed by the staff was a constituent part of the Rail-War Operation, and they proposed the coordinated sapping of dozens of bridges in order to achieve a very long-term, comparatively speaking, paralysis of the entire transport system of the enemy. Well, it would have been considerably harder to rebuild the bridges than to repair a railroad on land after blowing up a train. Based on the project worked out by the brigade staff, it was proposed to create a school for light sapper-divers, numbering up to 400 men. The graduates of the school would have to work underwater in IPA-1 and IPA-2 oxygen equipment, be familiar with mines and explosives, carry firearms and sidearms, and possess skills in hand-to-hand combat and parachuting.

It was proposed that saboteur divers be thrown into the enemy rear at the location of partisan brigades, and they would then, accompanied by divers, set out for the intended objectives and carry out their assigned missions.

This plan was coordinated with the specialists and received the approval of Central and Byelorussian Headquarters for the partisan movement.

The match is interesting, however, between the details of this plan and those of the operation already described, Khokhlov's blowing up the bridge across the Dnepr in 1943. In both places, a Spetsnaz group was trained and dropped to the partisans by parachute. In both cases, the soldiers went out with local divers to the sabotage site, executed the military mission, went off again to the partisan location, and from there were evacuated to the "homeland."

Which of these was the first and which the second? Was Khokhlov's operation the implementation of Tavrikov's, or was the plan set up on the basis of Khokhlov's successful experience? This is not clear and it's probably not all that important.

Something else is important: the plan to create special units of combat swimmers was not destined to materialize. The defeat of the German Army at the Kursk salient and the attack of Soviet forces into Byelorussia itself made the notion of an "underwater war" unfolding in the territory of Byelorussia a moot point.

This is practically all there are, more or less, of reliable histories about our sabotage-recon diver groups and simply of divers' skirmishes with the enemy, even though, as already stated, cross-referenced documents confirming them, other than those of RON operations, have not yet been found.

It's impossible not to mention, perhaps as an oddity, one more story that occurred, at the very beginning of the war, in August-September of 1941, in the words of the author Aleksandr Cherkasov, which he described in his book *The Defense of Odessa: Pages of Truth* (Odessa, Izd. Optimum, 2006) in the chapter entitled "The Soviet 'Torpedo' Men Attack."

The author describes in detail how at the beginning of September 1941, after long training, four groups of combat swimmers were thrown in two submarines into areas captured by the Germans at the Bulgarian ports of Burgas and Varna. Using two-seater, manned Del'fin torpedoes, with 660-pound charges of an explosive substance in their separatable bows, special waterproof suits for the combat swimmers, and oxygen breathing devices, the divers left the submarines through the torpedo tube, penetrated through the boom barriers to the port waters, and blew up their intended targets. As a result of blowing up the ships, oil and fuel poured out over the water and burst into flame, and then the detonation of ammunition began in various ships standing in port. The Germans lost six ships, sunk, and eleven damaged. In addition, the moorages in the port city of Burgas were destroyed to a great extent. Admiral Schiwind [*sic*], who commanded the German naval forces on the Black Sea [*Translator's note*: Admiral Schniewind was chief-of-staff of the *Seekriegsleitung* [Maritime Warfare Command] in 1941], wrote in a report to *Großadmiral* Raeder, who was in command of Germany's Navy: "The ships located in the port of Burgas sustained significant damage due to intruders. An air of flippancy has been exhibited, expressed in the underestimation of enemy capabilities ... the ports of Varna and Burgas are essential to our fleet, in the highest degree."

Unfortunately, of the eight combat swimmers, only three returned to Odessa. From then on, due to the situation developing on the land fronts, planning for sabotage operations was scaled down, a detachment was disestablished, and its equipment was evacuated to Sevastopol.

Even though in the beginning of the war, our oxygen-breathing apparatus was at least no worse than that of the Italians or the Germans, at that time, in general, there were no domestic underwater delivery vehicles, and those such as described in the book, even less so. Even if it is supposed that our guys had been able to scare up four Italian Maiale manned torpedoes, which there is no mention of at all in the literature, those torpedoes could not exit through torpedo tubes. The Italians set up special containers for transporting them on the decks of carrier boats (Fig. 018). So this is either a daring fantasy or an artistic invention.

Fig. 018: Italian Maiale manned torpedo, the only one of its type at the start of the war. With such dimensions, there was no question of fitting it into a torpedo tube.

Another story by I. Oskol'skiy appears in his book *The Heroic Deeds of Divers* (Sevastopol, 1994):

> A Soviet force, after freeing left-bank Ukraine from its Fascist invaders, decided to force the Dnepr on the march. But they did not succeed with this idea anywhere. On the right bank of the river, Hitler's pals had built a strong protective bulwark. To the north of Kiev, particularly heavy battles were rolling through in the region of Vyshgorod–Lyutezh. It was impossible to approach this bridgehead toward the Dnepr; the water in the river was boiling with the explosion of bombs, mines, and shells. In this very difficult circumstance, the front-line command authority decided to use a detachment of divers to secretly force the Dnepr.
>
> They selected physically strong, tall divers, gave them oxygen devices to wear, and equipped them well, and in the dark of night they set out along the river bottom for the right bank, which the Fascists had captured. There they succeeded, without firing a single shot, in killing the Fascist soldiers sleeping in trenches, in hand-to-hand combat, and giving the signal to the army strike force.
>
> Thus with minimal loss of personnel, the Dnepr was forced in the direction of Lyutezh. All the divers in the detachment were awarded decorations and medals, while the high title of Hero of the Soviet Union was conferred on their commander, P.Ye. Filonenko.

> Petr Yevdokimovich Filonenko graduated from diving school in 1934. He served for many years in the sapper forces. He learned to use light-diving oxygen equipment expertly and taught sapper soldiers to use it. And this learning stood them in good stead when forcing the Dnepr.

A check of the archives showed that a Capt. Petr Yevdokimovich Filonenko was there on the same duty, and he was actually awarded the title of Hero of the Soviet Union for crossing the Dnepr River. But, on the award citation for Hero of the Soviet Union (Fig. 019) the Capt. Filonenko mentioned by Oskol'skiy in this story is not there. He received this title for crossing the Dnepr, but not for diving activities—for organizing the crossing on auxiliary means.

But in light of the information presented earlier about "underwater infantry" operations on the Voronezh Front, this story, although not confirmed by an independent source, does not seem so fantastic.

So, what do we have, on the whole, with a focus on sabotage-recon divers in World War II?

Both before the war and in wartime, in both army and navy commands, there was a clear understanding of the potential for creating and utilizing light divers for purposes of sabotage and reconnaissance. A very large number of sources confirm this independently of one another.

If the sequence of actions is drawn up for those previously laid out by army specialists in their attempts to use light-diving equipment for military purposes, then an interesting picture takes shape:

> **Beginning of the 1930s**: a diver demonstration in the RKKA Corps of Engineers of a major capability for using light-diving gear to conduct military operations underneath the water.
> **End of the 1930s**: the creation of diving units in RKKA military districts, trained to secretly move people and military materiel over the bottoms of rivers and reservoirs and to conduct military operations, emerging onto land from under the water.
> **1941**: repeated attempts to create a unit of soldiers numbering hundreds of men, with the soldiers trained to work in light-diving equipment.
> **1942–1943**: individual sabotage and recon operations by light-diver soldiers at crossings and in the enemy rear.
> **1943**: plans were only mentioned for creating, within the complement of the Corps of Engineers, a special brigade of divers, numbering 3,800 men in all, who would go through light-diver training and were intended for conducting military actions in waterways, in nearshore zones, and in the enemy rear.

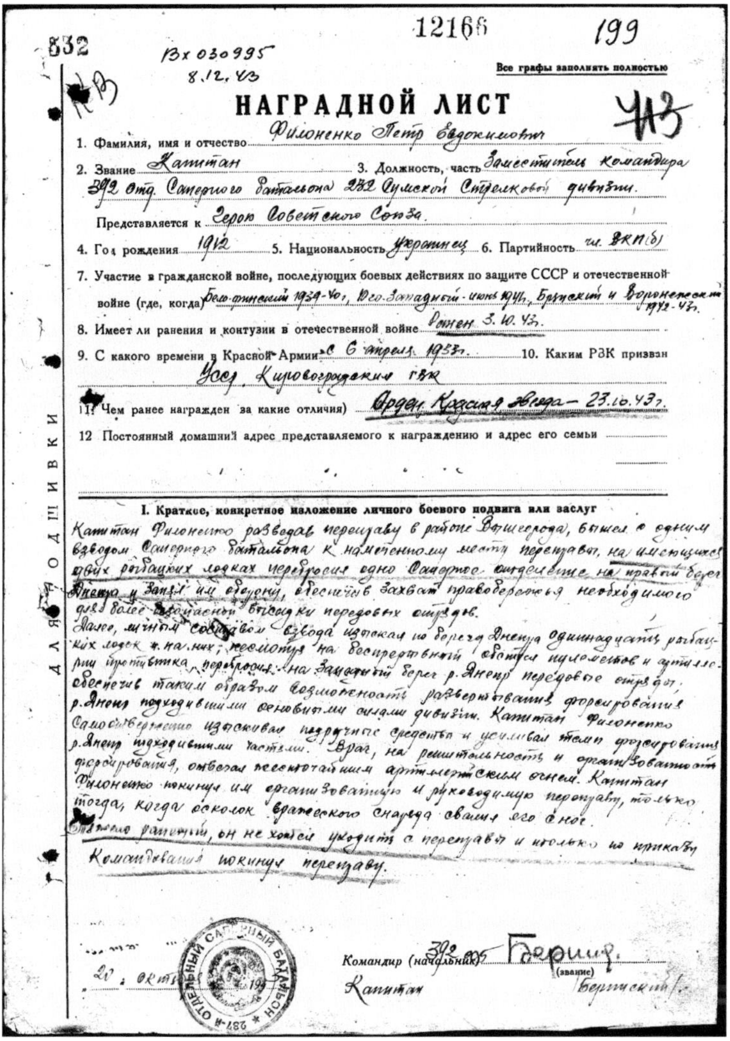

832 12166 199

Вх 030995
8.12.43

Все графы заполнять полностью

НАГРАДНОЙ ЛИСТ

1. Фамилия, имя и отчество Филоненко Петр Евдокимович
2. Звание Капитан 3. Должность, часть Заместитель командира 392 отд. Саперного батальона 232 Сумской Стрелковой дивизии.

Представляется к Герою Советского Союза.

4. Год рождения 1912 5. Национальность украинец 6. Партийность чл. ВКП(б)
7. Участие в гражданской войне, последующих боевых действиях по защите СССР и отечественной войне (где, когда) Бело-финский 1939-40 г., Юго-Западный - июнь 1941 г., Брянский и Воронежский 1942-43 г.
8. Имеет ли ранения и контузии в отечественной войне Ранен 3.10.43 г.
9. С какого времени в Красной Армии с 6 апреля 1933 г. 10. Каким РВК призван УССР, Кировоградский ГВК
11. Чем ранее награжден (за какие отличия) Орден Красная Звезда — 23.10.43 г.
12. Постоянный домашний адрес представляемого к награждению и адрес его семьи

I. Краткое, конкретное изложение личного боевого подвига или заслуг

Капитан Филоненко разведав переправу в районе Вышгорода, вышел с одним взводом Саперного батальона к намеченному месту переправы, на имеющихся двух рыбацких лодках перебросил одно Саперное отделение на правый берег Днепра у [illegible] им обороны, обеспечив захват правобережья необходимого для более безопасной высадки передовых отрядов.

Далее, личным составом взвода изыскал по берегу Днепра одиннадцать рыбацких лодок и на них, несмотря на беспрерывный обстрел пулеметов и артиллерии противника, перебросил на западный берег р. Днепр передовые отряды, обеспечив таким образом возможность развертывания форсирования р. Днепр подходившими основными силами дивизии. Капитан Филоненко самоотверженно изыскивал подручные средства и усиливал темп форсирования р. Днепр подходившими частями. Враг, на решительность и организованность форсирования, отвечал несмолкаемым артиллерийским огнем. Капитан Филоненко покинул им организованную и руководимую переправу, только тогда, когда осколок вражеского снаряда свалил его с ног. Тяжело раненый, он не хотел уходить с переправы и только по приказу Командования покинул переправу.

20 октября 1943

Командир (начальник) 392 ОСБ Капитан (звание) [подпись] /Берницкий/

287-й ОТДЕЛЬНЫЙ САПЕРНЫЙ БАТАЛЬОН

ДЛЯ ПОДШИВКИ

Fig. 019: Citation for Hero of the Soviet Union, awarded to Capt. P.Ye. Filonenko. (From the document bank *Heroic Deeds of the People in the Great Patriotic War, 1941–1945)*

1943: plans, worked out by the staff of the Plamya Partisan Brigade and approved by Byelorussian and Central Headquarters of the partisan movement, for creating underwater sabotage-recon groups in a complement of 400 men, equipped with IPA-1 and IPA-2 oxygen apparatus and specially trained for sabotage operations in the enemy rear.

It seems that light-diving equipment was proposed to be used in all these plans for clandestine penetration into the enemy rear, while the main military actions were to be carried out on land. This tactic is somewhat reminiscent of the actions of the Naval Infantry, which also lands on shore from the sea and also executes military actions on land.

It may be said with sufficient confidence that the issue the creation of regular units in the underwater "riverine" infantry, but in the army it was able to conduct several operations, in the best case, using divers, and almost all the those, with few exceptions, were random skirmishes with the enemy.

The situation in the navy turned out differently. The Red Banner Baltic Fleet brought this idea to systematic implementation when they created, and what is no less important, successfully utilized for their primary purpose, a specialized unit, a specops company of the reconnaissance detachment in Baltic Fleet Command.

The reason for such differences is probably in their "business as usual" thinking. Sailors were accustomed to have duty on the water, and the idea of them setting out against the enemy from under the water was psychologically acceptable; indeed, submarines do just that, in the final analysis. And a "diver" for a fleet command was a conventional concept. And it's just one step from the use of submarines to utilizing diving equipment for approaching the enemy in secret. And from there to the appearance of the RON, and post-war recon points in the main waters of navy responsibility, and Underwater Sabotage Forces and Resources (PDSS) units at naval bases.

The situation is different for an army command. The only ones who consider the water, more precisely water obstacles, as a location for their activity are the engineering units. But there are no engineers in the higher command structure of the army. On the other hand, in the initial period of the war, the situation was so complicated that there was no command for tactical frills, while after 1943, the war was rolling so rapidly westward that a real need for such formations did not even seriously arise: they were managing anyway. Only after the war did they return to the idea of creating specialized units in force structures that would have diving equipment, above all, and that would be capable of carrying out sabotage and reconnaissance activities from under the water. These are the well known Alpha and Vympel [*Pennon*] units, the specops units of the Main Recon Administration (GRU), and the like.

But during World War II, an army Spetsnaz diver remained, after all, exotic.

Chapter 3

THE NEAR-FRONT ZONE

A second group of events in which divers were directly affected by enemy firepower was that of providing crossing operations during military land-based actions and providing landings at sea. Practically any crossing or any landing, be it during an attack or a retreat, was a piece of cake for the enemy: they fired and bombed both crossings and landing craft unmercifully.

Usually, a landing or a crossing during an attack is a comparatively brief action: the troops pass on, the landing or crossing zone is no longer in the zone of effective enemy fire, and normal operations begin on building temporary bridges, constructing moorages for unloading ships, salvaging sunken property and equipment, and so on. But from the point of view of diving operations, there is a certain difference between divers securing crossings and securing landings, especially in the initial stages. At crossings, this difference is mainly in hydraulic-engineering operations, and during a landing, it is ship repair, and secondarily the construction of temporary moorages for unloading military equipment. And then later, as the enemy is pressed back, work begins on setting up loading and unloading zones, as well as for salvaging equipment and flotation means that were sunk during the landing.

Crossings

It has already been noted that crossings under enemy fire are comparatively short-lived. However, fords crossing the Neva in the region of Nevskaya–Dubrovka and those across the Volga in the Stalingrad region were unique. The crossing at Stalingrad operated for almost half a year, and the one across the Neva for a little more than two years, and all that time they were under direct artillery fire and bombardment. Lives were inevitably lost under enemy fire, equipment and military loads went down to the bottom, and diving operations at these crossings were being made continuously, even in the winter when there was ice on the Neva and the Volga.

But here is more detail about this: these crossings merit it.

Nevskiy Pyatachok

In September 1941, the Leningrad Front engaged in a landing across the Neva in the region of Nevskaya Dubrovka (Fig. 020). Its main mission was to prepare for breaking the blockade of Leningrad, which at that time happened to be ringed by German troops. Much has already been written, and in detail, about the landing itself and the heroic and tragic fate of our troops at the bridgehead on the left bank of the Neva. So we shall dwell only on the aspects of that operation that are associated with diving operations.

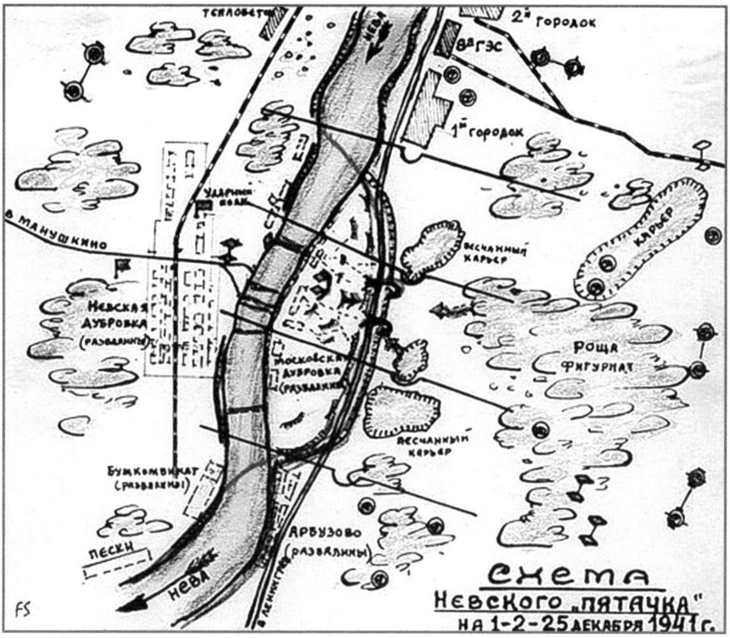

Fig. 020: Map of the Nevskaya Pyatachka bridgehead. Here we are, on the left, on the right shore of the Neva River, with the Germans on the right, on the left shore. (From the collections of the Museum of the Izhorskiy Factories)

The basis of any landing across a water obstacle is a crossing that is organized and clearly worked out. Rear Adm. F. Krylov, the head of EPRON, Maj. Gen. I. Fadeyev, and Lt. Col. B. Bychevskiy, head of the Corps of Engineers, were directed by Leningrad Front Command to lead the crossings from the right bank onto a "five-kopeck-sized" piece of land (a "pyatachok") at Nevskaya Dubrovka. The emergency rescue service group maintained the fords across the river; it included divers from a separate detachment of a Spetsnaz underwater operations outfit, separate from the EPRON complement (which by that time had been handed over to the navy), as well as divers from other units, such as RON divers.

Eight crossings were organized in all, but the heavy equipment, the tanks and artillery, traversed the Neva in the region of Nevskaya-Dubrovka, where there were sufficiently suitable approaches to the water (Fig. 021). The conditions for diving operations on the River Neva were complicated. The width of the river there was 886–1,148 feet, the depth was up to forty-nine feet, the current velocity reached 5 ft./sec, the temperature of the water varied by 68°F in the summer and dropped to practically zero in the winter. The bottom in the crossing area was compact sand with pebbles, but on the slopes, whose gradient reached 104–113°, it was silty sand. The water was turbid. Visibility under the water was almost nil, but that was not so important:

Fig. 021: The Neva River in the crossing region at Nevskaya Dubrovka. (Photo: December 7, 1941, from the TsGAKFFD collections, St. Petersburg)

the crossing place was in the enemy's direct line of sight and it was under fire, so that the divers had to work mainly at night.

The serious danger for a diver was not the diving conditions, however, but the artillery fire and bombardment of the crossings while a diver was underwater. And this danger accompanied the divers wherever they were under enemy fire, whether in the Volga in the Stalingrad region, at Sevastopol, on the Road of Life on Ladoga, in the Gulf of Finland where Kronstadt was being shelled, and a whole lot of other places—it's impossible to count them all.

Crossings were made on both sides. Equipment, weapons, ammunition, food products, and people crossed from the right bank to the bridgehead, in this case to the Nevskiy Pyatachok, and broken-down equipment and the wounded went back again. In order to reduce losses from enemy fire, a smokescreen was often used (Fig. 022).

Every possible flotation means was used for the crossings: boats, floats, and pontoons. In just the first stage of landing debarkation onto the left bank, thirty tenders and motorboats from the Ladoga Military Flotilla, ten boats, and 2,200 wooden sapper boats manufactured by the Leningrad factories were operated. A significant portion of the loads and people being transported across succumbed to continuous enemy artillery fire, and the smokescreens that were attempted in order to hide the crossing sections from enemy observation were far from always a help. The main task of the divers under these conditions

Fig. 022: Laying a smokescreen at a ford across the Neva River in the region of Nevskaya Pyatachka. (Photo: V.S. Tarasevich, 1941, from the TsGAKFFD collections, St. Petersburg)

was to search for and salvage sunken equipment, loads, and the actual flotation means of crossing, principally pontoons.

A welding repair shop was fitted out close to the river in a gulley. At night, the divers strapped up sunken pontoons, and then pulled the pontoons out onto the shore into the gulley with armored recovery vehicles and winches. In the daytime, they repaired them and then put them into action again.

Considering that every crossing was being watched and fired on by the enemy, Krylov proposed pulling the tanks and artillery over the Neva bottom using cables, snatch blocks, and manual winches. Testing the idea, done by actually pulling a tank over the bottom of the river at the EPRON base at the village of Rybatskoye, demonstrated its efficacy. A tank onshore can easily pull another tank over the bottom of a river. But doubts remained: the bottom of the Neva in the crossing area was strewn with sunken equipment, and the constant shelling raised doubts as to the possibility of keeping the cables in one piece. In the end, they decided to have the tanks cross in the usual manner: at night and under cover of a smokescreen on pontoons. But as an experiment, they decided to test pulling one heavy KV tank across the Neva. EPRON riggers stretched a cable across the Neva along the bottom and belayed it on a broken-down KV, which had to be returned to its own side for repair. They pulled the tank, but enemy shells broke the cable

Fig. 023: KV-I tank, raised in 2003 by the Belarusian Patriotic Military Club "Poisk" [Search], with the assistance of St. Petersburg searchers and divers. A tank emerging on shore looked roughly like this, after having been pulled over the bottom of the Neva at the ford at Nevskaya Dubrovka. (Photo: B.B. Sergeyev, *Search Command,* "Otkritoye More ["The Open Sea"], 2003)

eighteen times, and each time they had to start over again. Even so, the tank finally got to the other side, but it took ten days to do it (Fig. 023). In the end, they decided to only pull heavy equipment sunk in the process of crossing by dragging it over the bottom. There simply was no other way to get it out, in that case.

Two problems usually arose when dragging equipment over the bottom: breaks or snags in the cable and obstacles on the bottom. In both cases, divers freed the cable of snags, belayed it again, and strapped on obstacles found for subsequent salvage; these might be a sunken dinghy or boat, a pontoon, or even tanks and other military equipment that had gone to the bottom along with pontoons. On average, a diver in ventilated gear took up to forty minutes to eliminate a snag or to strap in an obstacle, under practically constant enemy fire and, as a rule, he came out of the water bruised to some extent.

In the end, crossing along the bottom was not the success anticipated, but several tanks, including two heavy KV tanks, managed to be pulled across all the same.

In the main, equipment crossed on pontoon ferries (Fig. 024), but in spite of cover, they often sank under artillery fire. Divers used soft ship-salvage pontoons to raise them and the equipment being transported on them. After inflating them with air, the pontoons floated to the surface with the load attached to them, and they were dragged, using winches, away to our shore. Sometimes, they hooked

Fig. 024: Construction of a ferry for heavy KV tanks crossing at Nevskaya Pyatachka. Inset: tank on a ferry. Unprotected under enemy fire, the tanks looked roughly like this on ferries at Nevskaya Pyatachka. (Photo: V.S. Tarasevich, 1941, from the TsGAKFFD collections, St. Petersburg)

a tug cable behind the sunken equipment and they pulled it by dragging it along the bottom with armored recovery vehicles. On shore, other recovery vehicles picked them up at the water's edge and whisked them off to Bol'shaya Roshcha.

Thus, the task of the divers in thcsc situations was to lay tow paths along the bottom of the river, clear the bottom of any obstacles (such as sunken logs carried along the bottom by the current or previously sunken pontoons and the loads they were transporting) in the movement corridor for an object being towed, whether a tank or a gun, and to restore broken tow cables.

When winter came and the river was covered with ice, crossing was done directly on the ice. But the ice broke apart under fire and equipment went to the bottom. And divers went into the water again and searched for and strapped up sunken tanks and guns. But to the nighttime darkness, with the cold water, the fast current, and the artillery shelling, were added grim frosts, and in the winter of 1942–1943, the air temperature fell to minus 77-86°F.

The divers knew that this meant going into water colder than minus 68°F. Air hoses froze, ice formed in them, which occluded air flow to the diver, and the hoses had to be heated up with boiling water. All wet and just coming out of the water, a diver's blouse turned to a block of ice in the cold, and, first taking away the helmet's porthole from a diver coming out of the water, they loaded him onto a sledge

Fig. 025: Heavy KV-I tank, raised in 2003 by searchers from the bottom of the Neva in the region of the Nevskaya Pyatachka crossing, restored at the Tank Repair Factory in Strel'na, and set up on open ground at the Breaking Through the Leningrad Blockade Museum and Preserve.

and dragged him to a warm place where he could strip down. Such "ice" baths were no gift to the divers.

Not everything that went to the bottom of the Neva at the crossings in the Nevskaya–Dubrovka region managed to be salvaged in those years, and to this day equipment lies on the bottom of the Neva that sank in the years of 1941–1943.

The Otkrytoye More [Open Sea] Search Command found a heavy KV-I tank in 2002, and in March 2003, searchers in the Belarusian Patriotic Military Club "Poisk," together with their St. Petersburg colleagues, pulled it ashore (Fig. 023). It had stood on the bottom, settling in three to five feet of bottom soil, and alongside it, at a dozen meters or so, was found the pontoon on which the tank was being transported. The pontoon was made up of four huge open iron boats, connected by welded rails at the top of the sides into a single whole. The pontoon had been flushed of soil, the bows of the boats had gone deep into the shoreside slope, the stern portions stuck out above the surface of the bottom, and it was even possible to climb into them. A lot of logs were stacked around the pontoon. The pontoon and the tank had apparently managed to cross most of the way at night or under cover of a smokescreen when the cable along which the pontoon was moving was broken by an exploding shell and the pontoon's hull damaged. The broken-down, sinking pontoon broke off from the cable and was carried downriver, and the tank slipped off the already sinking pontoon.

Later, in almost the same place, the searchers also salvaged one more tank, a BT-7 and yet another KV-I tank in 2011.

The salvaged tanks were restored and set up in a memorial park in front of a diorama at the Breaking through the Leningrad Blockade Museum and Preserve, which is dedicated to the breaking of the enemy blockade, on the right of Mariinskiy Bridge across the Neva (Fig. 025).

The Battle of Stalingrad

Military actions on the Volga before and during the battle of Stalingrad were both similar to what took place on the Neva in the area of Nevskaya Dubrovka and significantly different from it.

On the whole, in the Stalingrad region during the battle of Stalingrad, the situation in Volga waters was to a certain degree similar to the situation on the Neva, and in both places, the crossings were in the enemy's direct line of sight and under continual bombardment and artillery fire.

Everything that happened in the Volga channel above and below Stalingrad, i.e., beyond the limits of direct contact with the enemy, resembled more the situation on the Ladoga Road of Life: the Germans bombed and sank our ships with military cargoes for a considerable distance along the Volga; more about this a little later.

Beginning in August 1942, from the instant the Germans emerged on the Volga and the beginning of the fighting in Stalingrad, the crossings across the Volga became the only way to communicate with the troops leading the fight on city territory. Work on the crossings required a huge effort and a lot of courage. During the course of the entire battle of Stalingrad, the Germans conducted massed shellings of the channels, as well as of the boats, launches, and tugs with barges that were crossing the Volga. Volga crossings, either by day or by night, proceeded under heavy enemy fire. For instance, on one day alone, the twenty-sixth of October, and on only one channel at Bannyy ravine, the Germans dropped about 100 bombs, laid up to 130 mines, and launched more than 120 artillery shells.

For three weeks, October 7–28, they hit and burned or sank nine steamships and seven barges; thirty-five half-pontoons from the N-2-P fleet were damaged.

But in spite of that, work on the crossings did not stop. Divers from the emergency rescue detachments of the navy and the Riverine Fleet Narkomat played a significant role in the maintenance work

Fig. 026: Fords across the Volga River, whose width in the region of Stalingrad was a little less than a kilometer, were under constant enemy fire. (Photo: 1942, from the collection of the State Archives of Volgograd Oblast)

on the crossings and keeping the military loads and equipment being transported across the Volga. In the process of crossing, soldiers were lost with their personal weapons, and boats and barges with heavy weapons and ammunition, and so the main underwater operations consisted of salvaging sunken ammunition and weapons and clearing the bottom of the river at the sites for loading flotation means and offloading people and military cargoes (Fig. 027).

Dives were made, as a rule, in the nearshore belt of the Volga's left bank, and in areas in the enemy's direct line of sight, they were usually at night. The depths at the shore were not great, the bottom was flat and silty, the current got up to 1.6 ft./sec. Working conditions were not complicated, from a diver's point of view, but the continuous shelling made each dive verge on a heroic deed. During a dive under enemy fire, divers repeatedly received contusions and were even wounded.

All types of diving gear were used in the dives, both ventilated and lightweight: VIA-2 closed-circuit oxygen-breathing apparatus, a Series ShV mask-helmet, and Series E and TU-1 dry suits.

The results of these operations were simply astonishing and at times played a substantial role in maintaining the combat capability of our forces in Stalingrad. In August of 1942, for instance, a group of nine divers supporting the soldiers unloaded a barge sunk by the Germans, with 10,000 machine pistols on board in little more than a week. The automatic weapons salvaged were dried out and turned

Fig. 027: At the fords across the Volga River at Stalingrad, under enemy fire, our forces bore heavy losses. Divers in the crossing regions raised sunken military equipment and weapons, as well as the bodies of those who had perished. (Photo: 1942, from the collection of the State Archives of Volgograd Oblast)

over to the troops, who duly appreciated this gift. Another group of divers spent almost two weeks salvaging from another barge 2,720 cases of sunken shells, all of which had, by the next day, been fired at the Germans from Katyusha rocket launchers. Both weapons and ammunition salvaged at a crossing in this way went off on the spot to the troops and went into the fight.

But diving operations at crossings were not limited to extracting cargo from under the water or clearing out the bottom at loading and unloading sites. Divers also salvaged sunken ships and repaired the draft portions of hulls, as well as the screw and steering assemblies of ships still afloat.

With the war starting, a significant portion of the male divers went off to the front, and their place was taken by women who had gone through light-diver training at OSVOD courses before the war and at the beginning of the war period. There were 17 women at Stalingrad Emergency Ship-Salvage Detachment No.1 (ASO-1). They used light-diving gear when working on objectives. As a rule, women were not allowed to work in ventilated gear as it was too heavy (Fig. 028).

Women divers were "specialized" in searching for and salvaging cargo: weapons, ammunition, and other military equipment from cargo ships and military vessels sunk under enemy fire, as well as making minor repairs on ships afloat and clearing the approaches to wharf facilities at the sites of fords across the Volga.

Fig. 028: Female divers in Stalingrad getting ready for a descent (Photo: 1942(?), from the RGAKFD collections)

V.P. Kozlov, a diving specialist in the Podvodrechstroy, met with some of these women and wrote down their stories. Here is one of them from Dina Guseva (recorded in 1972):

> I was born in Stalingrad in 1922. I graduated from school and from the light-diving course at the same time, before the war. In the summers of 1940 and 1941, I worked as a

rescue diver: I was on duty at the city beach on the left bank of the Volga, which was at the little town of Bakalda. Time and again I had to save people from drowning. Not everyone could be saved. I carried the others in, to hand over to their relatives for burial. In short, I began to get used to working with the drowned.

But then, when the war began and Stalingrad became a city on the front line, it's impossible to express in words everything I saw and lived through. They assigned me and several other "OSVODers" to ASO-1, which had just been set up on the unloading dock at the local wharf. This was in August 1942. We girls and several of the lads then went through accelerated retraining to master the ventilated equipment. We passed the exam, and were put on duty right away.

The Fascist aircraft offered no possibility of working. In the intervals between the bombings, myself and some boy divers did ourselves proud underwater, extracting various equipment, including medical supplies from the passenger ships *Il'ich, Martyn Lyadov, Viktor Khol'zunov,* and *Petr Tschaikovsky.*

And everything we salvaged from the water, the delegate from Stalingrad Front Headquarters sent off with no delay, to be used as originally intended. We looked first of all for weapons and salvaged them: ordinary artillery shells, rockets for Katyushas, machine guns, automatic weapons and pistols from those killed, even rifles, binoculars, and medical supplies.

And later we began to recover the dead. There were an awful lot of them, but rarely anyone who was in one piece. They buried them here, on the shore.

That work was very hazard to health, in the sense disease control. We went down into the warm Volga in a light summer diving suit with no gloves. And when we came out and undressed, before long the skin on our hands was covered with spots and sores from the decomposing corpses. It wasn't just the boys who got that kind of work. But it had to be done, and we carried out our commanders' assignment. Personally speaking, my prewar OSVOD service on the Stalingrad beaches helped me a lot in that job.

I came back to the city where I was born, on the Volga, right after the war. But at that time I had entered military service on the Dnepr and the war ended in Germany. Yes, I had served by then in a different kind of military force.

Fig. 029: Equipment broken down at a crossing. A Soviet convoy at a river ford, destroyed by German aircraft below Kharkov, May 1942.

The Crossings, the Crossings ...

In the second half of the war, when the front line was rolling westward, our army had to force numerous water obstacles, and such big ones as the Dnepr, the Desna, the Bug. As a rule, divers were not used when seizing the forward portions of a bridgehead on a shore taken by the enemy, neither for sabotage and reconnaissance activity nor to support the forces and resources floating across.

After the capture of the bridgehead, their work was just beginning, with intensified transfer of troops and equipment to the opposite shore under artillery fire and enemy bombardment. The main task of the divers here was to clear out the bottom in the area where ferries and boats were being loaded and unloaded. But there were never ever enough divers in the pontoon-ferrying units, and the head of the Corps of Engineers in the 7th Guard Army pointed out the following in his response of December 31, 1943, to the head of the Corps of Engineers, 2nd Ukraine Front Command, concerning engineering support for the 7th Guard Army in forcing the Dnepr river (September 23 to October 26, 1943), including the organizational deficiencies of the operations: "The lack of proper provision of diving resources (one diving dress, in poor condition, for two battalions) ought to be considered serious neglect. The role and significance of the dive stations in reconstructing [Author: the pontoon] depot is very great."

Fig. 030: The ford across the Dnepr, under fire during the Lyutezh operation, 1943.

In fact, the work of the divers only began after the crossing area, along with the expanded bridgehead, were no longer subject to direct enemy action. Up to that time, emergency rescue detachments were hauled off to the crossing site, to protect the operations properly. On the whole, diving tasks differed little at that stage from the usual ones: surveying the bottom at the near shore portions of the ford, searching for and salvaging equipment and flotation means sunk during combat actions, etc.

That's how it was, for instance, when organizing rescue operations at a crossing over the river Dnepr during the battles to liberate Smolensk.

The formation of an expeditionary rescue detachment to secure operations for crossing the Dnepr was handed over to Z. Ye. Leybovich, whose commander assigned this task to him. At that time, Leybovich was a pre-eminent specialist in emergency rescue work, a veteran of the operations on the Road of Life and at Nevskiy Pyatachok.

The detachment was formed up in three days and fitted out with gear. It moved out to the operating area in eleven trucks and immediately set out to accomplish its mission. The detachment divers, like all of its personnel complement, rebuilt pontoon bridges damaged by shells and bombs and salvaged sunken military equipment, weapons, and flotation means (barges and boats) from the bottom of the Dnepr.

At the end of the fighting at Smolensk, the detachment remained in the crossing area, rebuilding destroyed bridges, clearing up the approaches to the crossing sites, constructing pontoon bridges, and effectively securing the movement of troops and materiel across the Dnepr behind the attacking units. The Germans periodically bombed the crossings, and the detachment divers had to search for and salvage equipment and weapons again and again, to clear the waterways, along which the movement of ships had begun, of sunken flotation means, mines, and fougasses [Editor: improvised mortars].

After Smolensk became beyond the enemy's reach and no one threatened the crossings any longer, the detachment was based on the Western Dvina and took part in reconstructing the railroad bridge across the river, which had been blown up there.

Divers carried out similar operations at all the crossings in the course of battle. It states the following in operations reports of the 6th Army on the Voronezh Front for August–September 1942: "A company of divers, operating within the Army structure, was utilized mainly to extract from the bottom of the river Don sunken materiel and resources. In August, the company pulled the following out from the bottom of the Don river: three half-pontoon floats, several motor vehicles with their loads, twelve boxes of ammunition, one vehicle with aircraft bombs, and other things."

And so it was, along all the crossings over great rivers on all the fronts.

Landings

No less significant, if no more complicated, was the work of divers in the complement of the emergency rescue groups that secured naval landings. Most of those were conducted in the Black Sea theater of operations. In the landing process, both landing craft and the rescue boats that supported them were under the enemy's direct precision fire from the shore. But in spite of this, the salvagers rendered extremely essential assistance to damaged landing craft, although they too sustained serious losses.

Capt. 1st rank V. Yurganov, the researcher on the history of the navy's emergency-rescue service, who was mentioned above, wrote:

> 1943. Lt. Capt. P.D. Vetov's ASO group secured the assault landing at Myskhako. Under enemy fire, the rescue divers took more than two dozen boats off the rocks, saved hundreds of the assault troops, and returned 283 ships supporting the landing, back into service. Completion of tasks on the coast that was under German control; A.N. Kuznetsov's group took a damaged DB-10 landing craft and a naval subhunter off the shoals.
>
> October–November 1943. Four emergency-rescue groups

(ASGs) secured a landing operation on the Crimean peninsula under gale conditions and heavy opposing enemy fire from land, air, sea, and at solidly mined defenses. The rescue forces saved twenty-seven assault landing craft, fourteen air defense (PVO) boats, twenty-three minesweepers, two torpedo boats, and twenty-eight fire-support boats. In the course of the rescue operations, forty-eight rescue divers and seven dive boats were lost.

It's hard now to imagine what took place in the waters and at the shore belt in the landing zones. Photographs from that time, often taken by Germans after our unsuccessful landings (and they occurred, unfortunately: the Kerch–Feodosiya landing operation of 1941, the landing at Southern Ozereyka, near Novorossiysk, in 1943, and several others) offer only a poor idea of what it was like. Well, even successful landings were accompanied by heavy losses in people, military equipment, and landing craft.

According to award citations for divers in the Black Sea Fleet, it's evident that they were right in the debarkation zone, and quite a lot of landing craft and motorboats were saved by their hands.

A few examples follow.

Diver 3rd Class V.P. Tatarenko, a Red Fleet sailor: "In the period of the Kerch landing operation in 1943–1944, he accomplished missions to construct moorages for landing craft at Kerch Bay. All his tasks were perfectly executed and in a timely manner, in spite of the action of enemy aircraft. There Comrade Tatarenko was wounded in the soft tissue of his right hip."

Diver 1st Class, G.I. Belousov, a petty officer: "In 1943, he took part in landing operations at Malaya Zemlya and at Myskhako. There he participated in constructing moorages for a tank crossing at Malaya Zemlya, which was under machine-gun fire and bombardment."

Diver 2nd Class A.D. Kuznetsov, a senior Red Navy sailor: "In the fall of 1943, he participated in diving support for landings of our forces with tanks at Kerch, where he dove underwater under enemy fire to render assistance to the boats."

Petty Officer V.K. Protsenko, Dive Command Petty Officer:

1. During the liberation of the city of Anapa, Comrade Protsenko, as the youngest commander, together with his complement of divers, executed missions in support of the boats during the assault landing, thereby demonstrating boldness, courage, and valor.
2. During the liberation of Taman and the Taman peninsula and during the conduct of landing operations on the Crimean shore

Fig. 031: A damaged naval subhunter stayed afloat and returned to base after a landing operation. It was precisely thanks to the divers that dozens of boats damaged in landing debarkations and their crews were saved.

in the Eltigen area, Comrade Protsenko supported the operations the entire time with unceasing work on the boats during the debarkation of the landing craft. Despite enemy fire and bombardment, he rendered assistance to boats that had suffered breakdowns.

3. After the period of the Anapa and Eltigen operations, under the leadership of Comrade Protsenko, fifty boats were raised, taken from the shoals, and repaired.

Senior MVP-2 Diver M.V. Perekrest, a senior Red Navy sailor: "He rendered assistance to ships taking part in landing operations and suffering breakdowns, including unwinding cable from and clearing the screws of the minesweeper Molotov and the small subhunter MO-107. Effectively supporting the operation, he afforded the damaged ships an opportunity to once again accomplish their military missions."

Operations in the near-front zone and diver support for crossings and landings were hardly the most dangerous type of diving work in all that was accomplished during the war. You had to have extraordinary courage to dive under direct enemy fire without weapons and unprotected and still perform your duty. Many of the divers died or were wounded, but their efforts helped to ensure the success of on-going operations, to bring dozens of ships and vessels out from under enemy fire, and to save the lives of hundreds, if not thousands, of ship crew and those in the assault landing.

Chapter 4

THE CLOSE REAR

If the soldiers of the RON and other sabotage-recon groups had to learn afresh a new application of their diving know-how, taking into account the specific nature of the activity facing them: making long-distance clandestine transits, working independently under water, swimming silently on the surface, or manually towing various loads on the surface and underwater, divers in the rear did the usual work of searching for and salvaging sunken objects, unloading sunken vessels and motor transport vehicles, hydraulic-engineering work. But they did these under combat conditions, subject to enemy shelling, bombardment, and so on.

In the rear but close to the front lines were the Road of Life in besieged Leningrad, the Volga channel and its waterways during the battle of Stalingrad, and fleet bases at Sevastopol, Novorossiysk, and Murmansk.

Mine Warfare

At the beginning of the war, the Germans broadly mined waterways, water routes, and ports, using bottom mines laid down by aircraft. For instance, in the period of July 23–31, 1942, alone, the Germans dropped more than 200 mines into the Volga, and the Volga was mined for a distance of 248 miles, from Kamyshin to Nikol'skiy, notably in areas where it was impossible to avoid the mines, in the narrows, at the bars, and so on. About 400 bottom mines were dropped at waterways at the approaches to Kronstadt, a huge number of them lay on the bottom at the approaches and in the bays of Sevastopol, and it was the same in many other places as well.

With the bottom mines lying on the bottom, the usual minesweeping techniques could not detect or disarm them. The explosives in the bottom mines had acoustic and magnetic sensors capable of determining the instant a ship on the surface passed into the zone where the mine could operate. The explosives also "knew how to count" and did not trip right away, the first time a ship passed over them, but only tripped after a previously set number of passages, five or six or so. They also had mechanisms to blow up the mine if it was lifted up. These were either a depth sensor that "told" the explosives what the pressure was and consequently that the depth was decreasing (meaning that the mine was being raised), or a photo element that "sensed" that the water around the mine was growing lighter, meaning that the mine was being raised to the surface.

The first models of non-contact mines dropped from aircraft were dropped by parachute, and the place where they were found was more or less obvious. Later the Germans began to use bomb-

Fig. 032: Minesweeper blown up by a bottom mine. (Photo: 1943, from the TsGAKFFD collections, St. Petersburg)

mines, which were dropped into the water without a parachute, and it was especially difficult to find those. Those and other mines lay on the bottom, where minesweepers ordinarily passed over them without grabbing hold. They had to be dealt with not by the ordinary trawl-sweep but in somc othcr way. Thc tcchnology for gctting rid of mincs with acoustic explosives was quite simple. Torpedo boats were sent into the zone where the mines lay, and they dragged this area at high speed many times. The mine "heard" the roar of the boat's engine passing above it, its delayed action was finally triggered, and the mine exploded, but due to the high speed of the torpedo boat, the danger zone was behind it. But sometimes, it was underneath the boat (Fig. 032).

But the subtlety of the situation was that not all the mines had an acoustic fuse, but a magnetic fuse, which was set to detect a large target, such as a destroyer, at a distance of up to ninety-eight feet, and it did not "sense" a torpedo boat passing above the mine. It was impossible to say in advance what type of mine the enemy had laid and to clear them from the ship route. Fleet command therefore set the minemen three tasks: to find the mines, to find a way to lift them to the surface, and after puzzling out the internal device, to find a means of countering such mines.

The difficulty was that after a mine had exploded while you were lifting it, you didn't know precisely what had caused the explosion:

the reduction in depth, the increase in the light intensity, or something else. The mine had to be disabled while still on the bottom, and again this was a task for a diver.

Searching for mines also fell to the divers, and there were several search methods.

In Kronstadt, a watch was set for the waters of the smooth Leningrad–Kronstadt sea channel. Since the mines fell slowly on parachutes, the observation watch positioned along the channel was successful in pinpointing where they entered the water. Then the divers went to work; these were soldiers from a specops company, as a rule. The divers went out to the area where the mine had fallen, searched for it visually by the usual method, in a line or spiral search, and when the mine was found, they marked the location with buoys. Then an inflatable pontoon was attached to the mine, it was inflated with air by hose from a safe distance, and the pontoon, with the mine fastened to it, floated to the surface. If the mine exploded during the float—good riddance! If it didn't explode, it was suspended below a specially fitted raft, towed to a safe place, and again, exploded there. The murky water of the Gulf of Finland made searches highly difficult, but even so, in the period of 1943–1944 alone, soldiers in the company tasked with disabling mines made 840 dives. It was noted many times in the award citations for RON soldiers that the award the soldier received was for getting rid of booby-trap mines.

But to simply blow up a mine of unknown construction was not enough. You needed to disarm it, to understand the operating principle of the fuses and create a means of countering it, with special sweeps to detect the mines and the application of safety measures for ships crossing in a mine's "field of vision." The first successes in disarming bottom mines were gained in the Black Sea, in the Sevastopol area.

On the Black Sea, where the Germans had displayed no less mining activity than on the Baltic, the search situation was simpler: the water was much more transparent and warmer, which facilitated a visual search.

Even at the very beginning of the war, divers were already finding bottom mines in Sevastopol Bay. But the very first mine exploded in an attempt to raise it. It became clear that the mines were fitted with self-destruction devices. A decision was made to disarm them directly underwater, since to simply blow the mine up was, as we said, not enough; we needed to understand the principles of its construction and to develop safety measures. This problem was posed to the fleet minemen, and its solution was handed over to Lt. Capt. G.N. Okhrimenko, a top officer and mineman in the OVR. A group of divers, equipped with nonmagnetic gear, was allocated, with him in command.

Fig. 033: Explosion of a bottom mine in Sevastopol Bay. (Photo: B. Sheynin, 1941, from the collections of the Central Armed Forces Museum of the Russian Federation)

At the end of June 1941, diver L.P. Vikulov found one of the latest mines and he led Okhrimenko to it. On June 27–28, Okhrimenko inspected the mine and removed its fuzes and delayed-action device in the course of several dives. But on the last dive, while he was underwater, Okhrimenko came under artillery fire, he was shell-shocked when he came to the surface, and he was not allowed to do any further work underwater. Divers carried out all the subsequent operations with the mine, and Okhrimenko had to guide them from the surface.

Then and later, taking into account the magnetic sensitivity of the mines, dives were executed from a wooden dive boat using nonmagnetic diving gear and a specially made nonmagnetic tool. There had to be a mineman on board the boat, in addition to the dive station, whom a diver could communicate with in the course of the activity.

Here is what I.I. Oskol'skiy writes about searching for and disarming a bottom mine in his book, *The Heroic Deeds of Divers*:

> Diver L.P. Vikulov worked along with the experienced mineman, G.N. Okhrimenko. They became intimately familiar with an unsophisticated device (a copper tube, glassed in at

one end). By looking through the glazed end of the tube lowered into the water, they quickly detected one of the mines, not far from the Konstantinov ravelin. It lay at a depth of fifty-two feet.

And the diver went into battle with it. First of all, he detached the parachute from the mine casing and lifted that to the surface. Then, on the mineman's advice, he studied the outer construction of the mine for a couple of hours, reporting to Okhrimenko in detail about what he saw.

On the second day, Vikulov, following the mineman's recommendations, took casts of the screws, bolts, and hatches. Based on these casts, antimagnetic tools were made.

On the third day, the diver set about the most dangerous operation in his life. He had to turn the screws and open the hatch cover. There was a possibility that the fuse might explode, and then.

The last screw turned. The hatch cover suddenly just popped right out of place and struck the diver hard in the chest. Vikulov blacked out for a moment from nervous tension. Falling, he managed to clutch at the cover, on the other side of which was fastened a spring. Coming to, the diver, with difficulty, surfaced.

The next day, Vikulov went down again. He gingerly approached the mine, carefully considered its internals through the open hatch, and proceeded to extract the hydrostat. Following Okhrimenko's advice, he neatly removed the inertial fuse and then the electrical fuse, and extracted the detonator, which was designed to amplify the action of the fuse. A cold sweat was running down into the diver's eyes, and his hands were reduced to cramping from the tension. But Vikulov found the strength to do everything the mineman suggested. And he won his four-day duel with the mine.

L.P. Vikulov received his first Order of the Red Star for disarming and raising the mine. He also received a second decoration for disarming a bottom mine, but by now that was a new model, dropped from an aircraft without a parachute and fitted with additional, novel booby-trap fuses that reacted to light. He carried out this operation in the waters of the Gelendzhik region, which was very close to Novorossiysk Naval Base.

At that time, they searched for mines using a different technology. In the morning, when there was fog over the sea and the enemy could not lay down precision fire, a dive boat went out into an area where there were supposed to be mines.

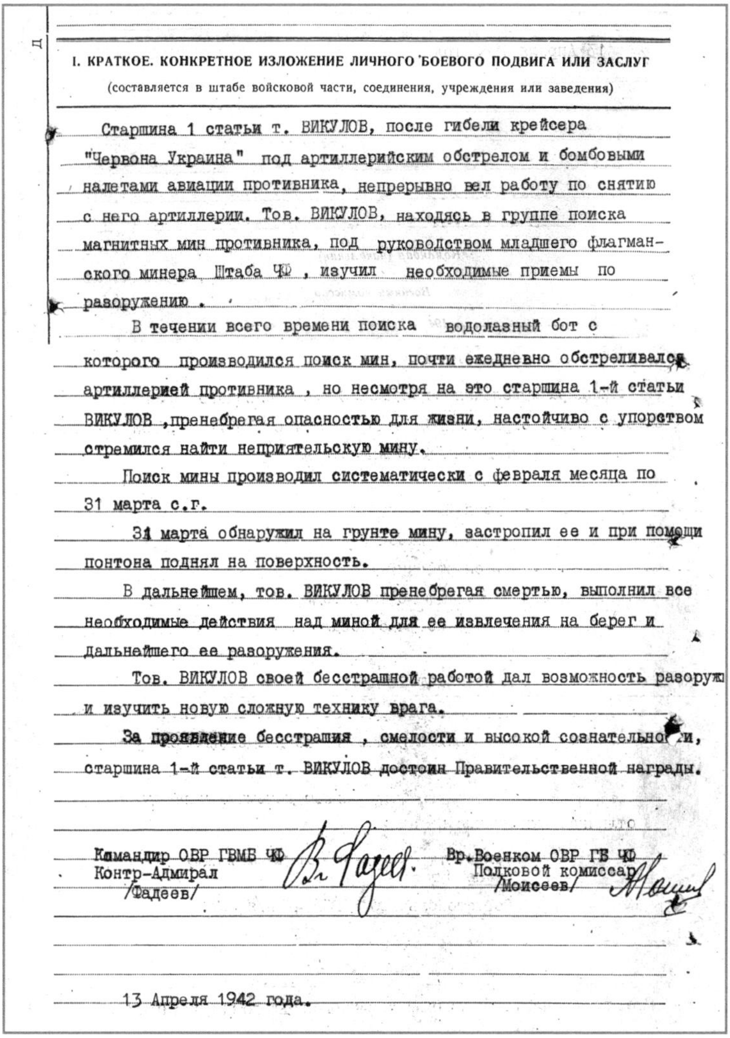

I. КРАТКОЕ. КОНКРЕТНОЕ ИЗЛОЖЕНИЕ ЛИЧНОГО БОЕВОГО ПОДВИГА ИЛИ ЗАСЛУГ

(составляется в штабе войсковой части, соединения, учреждения или заведения)

Старшина 1 статьи т. ВИКУЛОВ, после гибели крейсера "Червона Украина" под артиллерийским обстрелом и бомбовыми налетами авиации противника, непрерывно вел работу по снятию с него артиллерии. Тов. ВИКУЛОВ, находясь в группе поиска магнитных мин противника, под руководством младшего флагманского минера Штаба ЧФ, изучил необходимые приемы по разоружению.

В течении всего времени поиска водолазный бот с которого производился поиск мин, почти ежедневно обстреливался артиллерией противника, но несмотря на это старшина 1-й статьи ВИКУЛОВ, пренебрегая опасностью для жизни, настойчиво с упорством стремился найти неприятельскую мину.

Поиск мины производил систематически с февраля месяца по 31 марта с.г.

31 марта обнаружил на грунте мину, застропил ее и при помощи понтона поднял на поверхность.

В дальнейшем, тов. ВИКУЛОВ пренебрегая смертью, выполнил все необходимые действия над миной для ее извлечения на берег и дальнейшего ее разоружения.

Тов. ВИКУЛОВ своей бесстрашной работой дал возможность разоружи[ть] и изучить новую сложную технику врага.

За проявление бесстрашия, смелости и высокой сознательности, старшина 1-й статьи т. ВИКУЛОВ достоин Правительственной награды.

Командир ОВР ГВМБ ЧФ
Контр-Адмирал
/Фадеев/

Вр. Военком ОВР ГБ ЧФ
Полковой комиссар
/Моисеев/

13 Апреля 1942 года.

Fig. 034: Presentation of an award to Petty Officer L.P. Vikulov for finding and destroying a non-contact bottom mine at Sevastopol. (From the document bank *Heroic Deeds of the People in the Great Patriotic War, 1941–1945*)

From the boat, a bosun's chair was lowered with a diver seated on it who was slowly pulled along a couple of yards above the bottom. In the towing process, the diver looked over the surface of the bottom and found a mine, which they then blew up somehow or other.

This is how the participants in this operation describe diver Vikulov disarming a bottom mine in Gelendzhik waters:

> Looking at the bomb, he established that it had a special metallic housing, with instruments underneath it. Since a photo element might be one of the instruments, they decided to work at night.

Vikulov dove down and attached a long tow rope, which they used to yank the housing off the mine. The mine didn't explode. When the diver went down to it again, he found, by touch, a spherical device with little windows: those were the treacherous photoelements! For insurance, Vikulov wound the device in a lightproof cloth and only then removed it. Then he took out the inertial fuse and the detonators. The bomb-mine was safe.

Vikulov was awarded the Order of the Red Banner for this heroic deed.

To understand what a "dirty trick" these bottom mines were, here is a brief description of how Vikulov disarmed a German, Type G, bottom mine:

The bottom mine is dropped from an aircraft without a parachute. The casing is cylindrical with a spherical nose. The tail portion is shaped like a truncated cone. The stabilizer is made of plastic and smashes when it hits the water.

Tactical-technical Data:
- weight of the charge: 1,620 lbs.
- total length: 6.30 ft.
- diameter of cylindrical portion of the mine: 2.16 ft.
- depth of the landing site: 26–164 ft.
- drop altitude: no more than 328 ft.

Period of delayed action. Usually three, but could be any number up to fifteen.

Operating principle. A magnetic fuze is triggered by a change in the vertical component of the magnetic field at the landing site. A hydrostatic instrument switches on the mine circuitry at a depth of twenty-four feet or more, whereupon; pulling the mine out of the water causes it to explode. Booby-trap instruments. The mine has two booby-trap instruments, one to blow up the mine when the inertial fuze is pulled out, the other when the hood covering the apparatus is removed. Special considerations. Two photo elements operate in a magnetic-switch system, blowing the mine up when light falls on it.

As is evident from the description of the mine, the disarming process had multiple steps and was complicated. The booby traps were designed to blow the mine up at any attempt to deactivate it. Not a few minemen

Fig. 035: One of seventeen bottom mines found and disarmed by divers in the waters of Gelendzhik Bay.

died on shore while disarming mines already salvaged, and a lot of divers died while disarming mines on the bottom. Nevertheless, the secrets of these bottom mines were successfully revealed.

As a result of studying the principles hypothesized when the enemy designed the bottom-mine fuses, electromagnetic trawling sweeps were created to blow the mines up, and safety measures were developed based on demagnetizing ship hulls, thanks to which the magnetic mines did not "sense" ships passing overhead.

Several dozen non-contact mines in all, with various types of fuse (magnetic, optical, and others), were discovered and raised by divers in the waters of Sevastopol and Novorossiysk Bays. However, it must be said, that far from all of the mines were found during the war. Many of them are still lying on the bottom, and furthermore, the waves sometimes carry them onto shore. Not so long ago, they found such a mine on shore in Sevastopol, and in attempting to dismantle it, one of its booby traps blew apart, killing two men and injuring another. On average to date, one or two bottom mines are found after storms every year on the bottom and on shore near Sevastopol and along the Crimean shoreline, and they are destroyed.

Mines are found today, more than sixty years after the end of the war, in places other than the Black Sea. In 2008, upon finishing construction on the southern part of the Kronstadt dam, a dredge lifted up one of the previously mentioned aircraft bomb-mines. Another of these mines was found the same year in the Gulf of Finland at the edge of the waterway, right next to the pilot vessel *Petersburg*, which was being salvaged.

Leningrad, Ladoga: The "Road of Life"

Leningrad came under siege in the beginning of the fall. The Finns left for the city from the north, from the Karelian Isthmus, and the Germans from the west and south, cutting through the main communications, cutting Leningrad off from the rest of the country. The city had no power, no fuel, and no provisions.

The only section of the marshy shore of Lake Ladoga that was accessible to the defenders of Leningrad had no infrastructure of any sort: no automobile roads or railroads, no ports, no loading or unloading points, no bases or warehouses. And it was precisely through this section of the Ladoga shore that there had to pass into Leningrad provisions, military equipment and ammunition, soldiers, power, and fuel, and out of Leningrad the equipment from businesses being transferred westward and Leningrad citizens being evacuated: children, women, and old people.

This route across Ladoga, later called the "Road of Life" (officially named Military Highway No. 101), was the single link besieged Leningrad had with the rest of the country, by water in the summertime, over the ice in the winter, and over the bottom throughout the entire year, and it operated from September of 1941 through March of 1943

This route had to be built and put into operation, and quickly. The amount of time calculated for this was not weeks but days; the first winter of the blockade was at hand. As a result, it developed that divers had to apply all their know-how on the Road of Life on Lake Ladoga, in all types of activity, irrespective of the weather and the military situation: emergency rescue operations, hydraulic engineering construction, laying down communications (pipelines, electrical power cables, and voice communications).

The main volume of underwater work associated with the surface infrastructure of the Ladoga shore, in creating the Road of Life and supporting everything using it, lay with the EPRON divers, who were organized into detachments for underwater engineering and rescue operations and scattered among the principal ports and channels, as well as on the Road of Life route.

Beginning with the construction of a port at Osinovets in September 1941, by the end of 1942, divers had already worked on more than a hundred objectives such as: ports and port stations, underwater cables, underwater pipelines, the waterways for water routes, sunken vessels and barges, motor vehicles, military equipment, and much more.

Besides the EPRON divers (who were the navy's rescue service), divers from Specops Company, Recon Section, Baltic Fleet Command,

Fig. 036: Preparing a diver for a descent under the ice. (Photo from the collections of the Museum of the Defense and Blockade of Leningrad)

divers from the Ladoga Military Flotilla, and soldiers from the Red Army Corps of Engineers worked on the Road of Life.

And without the work of the divers, which was hard (both physically and morally, particularly when raising motor vehicles from the bottom that had fallen through the ice, with women and children in them who were being evacuated from the city), the work was made worse by enemy aircraft, the cold, and the penetrating wind in winter, and on top of everything else, hand-to-mouth hunger during the blockade: divers received 10.5 ounces of bread a day, a little groats [grain], and a dab of fat.

Infrastructure of the Ports

The meager possibilities that remained in our hands for that section of the Lake Ladoga shore limited the amount of cargo that could be transported by vessels; there were virtually no ports or loading and offloading capabilities on shore. And without these, there was no question of normal cargo turnover being possible. The first task assigned by Leningrad Front Command to the hydraulic engineers, then divers, that is, was to build up the Ladoga shore.

To solve this problem, a decision was made by the Military Front Council to involve the Baltic Technical Fleet of the USSR Narkomstroy, as well as EPRON (which had been handed over by that time into the navy structure), the Northwest Riverine Steamship Line, and the engineering units of the Leningrad and Volkhov Fronts.

Construction of the ports began simultaneously in the west (the area of Osinovets lighthouse, Gol'tsman Bay, and Mor'ye Bay), and in the east (at Kobon station and at the village of Lednevo) on the shores of Lake Ladoga.

The steps they took produced results. By the end of September 1941, two moorages had been constructed at Osinovets with a depth of eight feet, with two more moorages on Gol'tsman Bay with depths of 5.5-8 feet, and a protective dam erected at Mor'ye Bay. The moorages were connected by railroad spur lines to the main railroad route. Warehouses were built in the forest in the moorage area.

But since no ports or shelters were in operation yet, vessels had nowhere to hide from inclement weather, especially on the western shore; barges with cargo were torn away from their anchors and ended up on the nearshore rocks. An EPRON rescue party was able to get some of them off the rocks and tow them in semi-submerged condition for repair at Novaya Ladoga.

With start of winter, the tempo of operations intensified. Crib piers were made and set up for the moorages; the pilings were clogged with ice. Railroad access lines were laid at the moorages, and lift cranes were assembled.

The volume of work to be done with the limited capabilities of Leningrad builders and hydraulic engineers was simply colossal. To construct just the moorages at Cape Lisiy Nos alone, they had pre-assemble 130 log crib piers, fill them with broken rock, and transport them to the piers assembled for the specific moorages. The divers assembled the piers, working for hours day after day in the freezing water (Fig. 037).

The 218-yard long slip on Gol'tsman Bay was a unique structure, with railroad lines going out into the water, which were later used to bring cistern-tanks with liquid fuel delivered by tug from the western shore. At the base of the slip lay a "rock bed" constructed by the divers for the underwater section of the railroad line.

The construction of the port's physical plant was accompanied by the constant attack of German aircraft, and every time there was an air raid warning, the divers had to get out of the water immediately, take off their gear, and go into hiding.

Nonetheless, the wintertime construction bore fruit: the Ladoga water route went into full operation for navigation in 1942, and cargo

Fig. 037: Divers from the 27th EPRON Detachment during hydraulic-engineering operations in the Neva River, 1941–1942. (From the collection of the Naval Museum, city of Kronstadt)

passed into Leningrad in an unending stream. But bombing regularly destroyed the port facilities, and the builders, including the divers, had to constantly reconstruct them.

A second battle with hydraulic-engineering operations for the western shore of Ladoga was linked to the need to strengthen the moorages for loading T-34 tanks, which had to be carried over to the Oranienbaum bridgehead. Attempts to ferry tanks over the ice did not always end well (Fig. 038), and a new, more reliable means, was needed, particularly in the ice-free period.

Pontoon men and divers in the engineering forces of Leningrad Front, working on the broken ice, reinforced the pier and cut a channel through into the ice for the passage of barges with tanks. Noticing the activity at the moorage, the Germans intensified the shelling of this region, which did not make the divers' work any easier. But in spite of that, the loading moorage operated without interruption, and dozens of tanks were redeployed into the Oranienbaum area to the battle site.

Emergency Rescue Operations

All types of equipment for Leningrad headed across Lake Ladoga were targeted by Fascist aircraft. German aircraft bombed vessels on

Fig. 038: Raising a KV-I tank from Lake Ladoga. (Photo: V.G. Fedoseyev, 1942, from the TsGAKFFD collections, St. Petersburg)

the water route almost constantly, as well as at the moorages of Osinovets port. And not without result. On September 15, 1941, for instance, the enemy sank a number of vessels and barges, including two barges loaded with grain, which had been standing at the moorage. The task of the divers in the 27th Underwater Technical Ops (PTR) Detachment was to raise from the water, from the vessels and barges that had sunk, in addition to equipment, various materiel, and food products. The divers often had to solve problems that required non-standard approaches and considerable imagination.

This happened with the barges mentioned above, in whose holds were more than 3,000 tons of bulk wheat. At first they tried to pump the grain out of the holds from a depth of two meters using a centrifugal suction pump. But the pump blades crushed the grain. Then the divers began to scoop the wheat by hand, with buckets. But that wasn't labor; it was "salty tears." In a six-hour shift, one station diver could manage to collect less than twenty bags worth. Then the same divers proposed using a suction-dredge ejector built before the war for working with sandy soils underwater. Delivered from Leningrad, they set the suction dredge in the hold of the barge and led a discharge hose up to it from a hydraulic excavator, along with a suction hose, which fed the water with the grain in it to the surface into a special hopper. The water ran

Fig. 039: Raising grain from a barge sunk as a result of bombing. Diver underwater; in the background behind the gap in the ice, a manual diving pump and two pumpers near it. (Photo: V.G. Fedoseyev, December 1941, from the TsGAKFFD collections, St. Petersburg)

out through the reticulated bottom of the hopper and the grain remained behind. The system began to operate a couple of hours after it was set up, delivering more than ten tons of grain an hour, which was poured into bags and sent off to Leningrad. Two days later, two more suction-ejectors were delivered to Osinovets, which were set up on a second barge. Operations went on day and night, and the divers, released by that time, unloaded bags of flour and other products that were not amenable to using a suction dredge (Fig. 039).

In the fall of 1941, five steam tugs (including one lake boat) and forty-six barges in all sank in Ladoga due to bombing and gales. Only seven barges remained in service. Divers from EPRON and the Ladoga tech-area route who were raising cargoes from sunken vessels often had to work underwater during enemy aircraft attacks. Nevertheless, a significant portion of the loads could be saved from flotation means that had sunk in port.

After the motor road opened across Lake Ladoga on the ice routes, motor vehicles sank systematically, especially during the ice freeze-up and in the spring muddy season. After only the first two weeks of the Road of Life's operation, 157 motor vehicles sank beneath the ice, and after a total of two blockade winters, more than 1,100 vehicles sank; one out of every four.

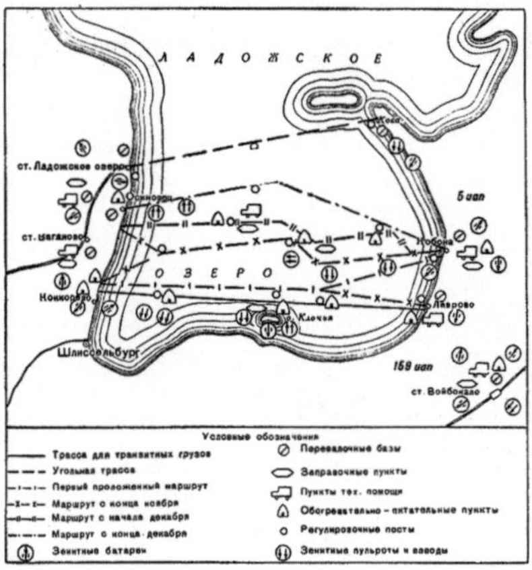

Fig. 040: Map of routes for the "Road of Life" on Lake Ladoga.

Fig. 041: Nearly everything was lifted using similar jacks: motor vehicles, guns from sunken vessels, boats sunk by the enemy, even tanks.

The EPRON craftsmen, who did the work on the routes, raised the sunken vehicles by hand, with a winch, using wooden jacks (tripods) and block and tackle (Fig. 041).

Raising motor vehicles, military equipment and cargo from the bottom was simplified as much as possible. The jacks stood on sled runners, they were pulled over to the lift site, set over the hole in the ice where a motor vehicle had sunk, and a diver went down to the bottom to strap the vehicle in. Then they lifted it to the surface with a manual winch, and they dragged the jacks, with the vehicle hanging on a hook, off to solid ice.

After a while, a vehicle that had been on the lake bottom was ready to carry loads again.

Every day, divers lifted onto the ice up to a dozen or more trucks, road construction machines, clamshells, snowplows, and tractors. In below-zero conditions, after working many hours in the water, the divers brought to the surface were not undressed right away. They were carted off to shore in their frozen suits. Only after being warmed up in a toasty place did they undress.

In one year, EPRON divers raised more than 3,500 tons of varied cargo, about 200 tanks, aircraft, and motor vehicles, 125 weapons and mortars, and more than 200 tons of ammunition.

Laying Cables for Communications and Electrical Power

The first cable line across Lake Ladoga, twenty-three miles long, was laid by the divers in the 27th EPRON Detachment by the fall of 1941. It was a communications cable provided to Leningrad Front Command for reliable communications with Moscow. But this was not a special under- water cable, and so the reliability of such a communications line was very low. Understanding this, the communications personnel immediately began to prepare to lay a special, multi-conductor, armored, underwater communications cable along the bottom of Ladoga, twenty-six miles in length and weighing 350 tons. To lay it, they needed to evaluate and select possible variants for a route, to perform engineering surveys along them, and, using divers, to inspect underwater obstacles that showed up during the surveys and to monitor the cable handling.

In spite of enemy shelling and bombing, the cable was laid, its position on the bottom was checked by divers over the entire route, and on October 29, 1941, the city had reliable communications.

Fig. 042: Raising the steam-driven tugboat Kama from a depth of forty feet. (Photo: March 1943, from the TsGAKFFD collections, St. Petersburg)

The next big operation laid on the divers' shoulders was the construction of five underwater, high-voltage cable lines to supply besieged Leningrad with electrical power from the Volkhov Hydrolelectric Station. The decision to begin the work was made by the Military Council of Leningrad Front on August 7, 1942. Specialists from the 27th EPRON Detachment were engaged to lay the cable on the bottom, as they already had similar experience, while for the assembly work their colleagues from the Lenenergo cable-grid sections were called on for assembly operations in splicing the separate sections of the cable into a single line and hooking it up to the grid. Two barges were used for the construction, with a tugboat and auxiliary tenders. A cable for the installation, with a total length of about sixty-eight miles, arrived in 1,640-foot sections. In the process of loading the cable onto the barge, its individual parts were joined into a single line and the splice was protected from the effects of the water by a special hermetically sealed collar (Fig. 43). The assembly of each component collar took six to eight hours, and the placement of the cable line, with a length of thirteen miles, into the hold of the barge required more than seven days, taking into account the assembly of about fifty-five collars.

Fig. 043: One of 228 cable sleeve-connections used to construct a cable line across Lake Ladoga. (Exhibit at the "Road of Life" Museum, settlement of Osinovets)

After completing the assembly of the collars and loading the cable, the barge set out onto the lake at night with the tugboat, and the cable was fed overboard as the barge moved along. The construction of the collars did not allow for any loads on them or any bends in the cable. And so, when the time came to lower the next connecting collar into the water, the auxiliary tender came up alongside the barge without stopping, the collar was reloaded onto the tender as it was moving, and then the tender backed away from the moving barge and stopped. The collar was lowered precisely onto the bottom, with a diver watching, the diver checked that it was lying on the bottom, and then the tender went up to the barge again and took up the next collar. The entire trip from shore to shore usually took fourteen to sixteen hours.

Divers buried the near shore portions of the cable in the soil of the bottom.

Five parallel cable lines were built in this way. The entire construction took about two months. The first line took up its load on September 23, 1942, the last, the fifth one, on December 7, 1942. All in all, electrical power coming into Leningrad was quadrupled by the end of 1942.

Over time, the cable lines constructed got covered over with sand and mud. In order to search for them for on-going cable maintenance, divers used an underwater route-finder produced by workers in the Lenenergo cable-grid sections (Fig. 044). A diver with an antenna walked along the bottom, and an operator on the dive boat determined the location of the cable in the bottom based on the level of the signal measured by the receiving unit.

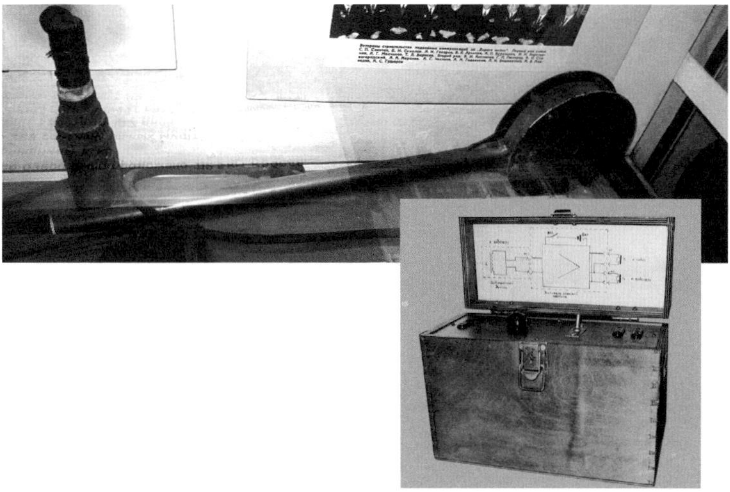

Fig. 044: Underwater line-tracer, built in 1942 in besieged Leningrad to search for electrical power and communications cables laid down on the bottom of Lake Ladoga. (Exhibit at the "Road of Life" Museum, settlement of Osinovets)

Laying a Gasoline Pipeline

After the closure of the blockade ring, German aircraft quickly put out of commission virtually all of our tanker fleet on Ladoga and from Leningrad itself, and the troops on the Leningrad front began to have an acute shortage of fuel. This problem had to be solved right away.

A way out was found. It consisted of cistern-tanks, ones already filled with fuel as well as empty ones, being floated on the water, and they could be towed afloat, built a little like a train, linked to one another. To implement this idea, divers on both shores of Ladoga built slips with railed tracks going out under the water to a depth of several yards, which in turn were connected to the main railroad line on shore. Tanks coming up to the shore reached the water on the slip rail lines, and divers in the water detached the undercarriages from the tanks and connected the tanks in groups of five to ten for subsequent towing. On the opposite shore, the tanks were set on undercarriages located above the slip tracks, and were attached to them, dragged onto the shore, formed up in the usual regular train, and hauled away as needed, either into Leningrad if on the western shore or for refilling if on the eastern shore.

But this method did not always work. In spite of air cover, the enemy periodically sank the tanks, and ice would be appearing pretty soon on the lake. The need had clearly arisen to construct an underwater pipeline that would not depend on weather or the time of year and would not be subject to enemy strikes from the air.

A decision was made to construct an underwater pipeline to supply the city with oil products (gasoline, kerosene, diesel fuel), and in the spring of 1942 preparations began for construction. Monitoring the construction preparations and the construction itself, as well as rendering necessary operational assistance to the builders, was entrusted to the authorized State Defense Committee for Leningrad under A.N. Kosygin.

Laying the pipeline was done by building it from the western to the eastern shore. It was welded on shore from individual pipes 19–29 feet in length to make sections of 656 feet each. After testing the seal of the joins and insulating the pipe against corrosion, these sections were dragged into the water from shore and, already floating, they were gathered into an assembly string 3,997–4,921 feet long. The first string began at the shore and its other end was anchored on the route. A second string, afloat at one end, was brought up to the first, and the join was welded and insulated. Joining the strings was accomplished by gas or arc welding on a separate pontoon float. The weld site was hidden behind special shields so that the weld arc would not reveal the location of the operations. After the joint cooled, it was insulated, the string attachment to the pontoon was released, and the pipe was lowered to the bottom. And so, step-by-step, they joined fifteen strings together into a line and laid it on the bottom, each with an average length of 4,593 feet. They welded the next string on the eastern shore, drew it into the water, joined it, afloat, to the last pipe, and laid it on the bottom. In the process of towing the strings, they were supported afloat by "pontoons" in the form of logs hung on the sides of the pipeline (Fig. 045). To sink the pipeline, the logs were simply chopped off, and the pipe went down to the bottom.

The time needed to fit and weld the strings to one another depended on the weather, but on average this work took three hours and twenty minutes.

All of the underwater work that had to be accomplished in laying the pipelines under water fell, of course, to the divers. They carried out surveys and mapping for a route sixteen miles in length at depths up to thirty-nine feet, they cleared the route of large rocks, snags, and other obstacles, and they prepared a trench in order to avoid sharp variations in depth along the route. Then, behind the caravan guiding the assembly of the pipeline, they went over the entire route again, assessing the condition of the submerged string and its position on the bottom. It was established that in the sandy sections of the route, the pipeline route was buried in the bottom to its full diameter. In areas where the banks were stony, there were places where the pipeline rose up eleven inches above the bottom, resting on rocks at individual points. In order to reduce the load on the body of the pipe at such places, rock supports were made underneath the pipeline, the supports being a distance of twenty-two feet apart (the length of a link of pipe).

Fig. 045: Assembling lashings for a pipeline: tying logs together to provide buoyancy. (Lake Ladoga, June 1942, photo from the collections of the History Museum of the Izhorskiy Factories)

To stabilize the pipeline in the near-bottom currents and surface waves, the divers attached the pipeline to the bottom using weights, which were set every 164 feet in depths of less than thirteen feet, and every 328 feet in depths of more than thirteen feet. Metal bars and a casting, each weighing 80-100 pounds, were used as the weights. The weights were connected in pairs by means of twisted wire nuts and were laid on the pipeline by the divers. The pipeline was reinforced by just such paired weights at each rock support.

The shore sections in the shallows (at depths up to five feet) were sunk 1.5 feet into the bottom using a hydraulic excavator.

After finishing the construction, the divers passed along the entire route once again and made sure that the pipe was lying close to the bottom, with no damage, bends or slackening.

Several dive stations worked on the route to speed up the construction, each on its own section. The daily norm of work for each dive boat (two dive stations), which consisted of cutting off logs, tracking the pipeline, attaching it to the bottom, and setting buoys, was 5,900 running feet.

In general, the divers did their customary work with "minor" exceptions, although they had to work under almost constant bombardment, at night, and at a furious rate.

The entire process of building the underwater section of the pipeline lasted from May 31 to June 14, 1942. After all the work was completed, they successfully tested the pipeline at an internal pressure of twenty atmospheres, and on June 17, 1942, it went into operation. The carrying capacity of the pipeline turned out to be equal to 300 tons of product pumped per day, and later, as experience accumulated, it reached up to 435 tons a day. This amount of fuel not only covered the city's and the army's current needs, but it allowed some reserve to be stored, calculating for an anticipated assault associated with breaking the blockade.

Many of those who took part received state awards for successfully completing the construction.

Let us note once again that the city, blockaded by the enemy, was linked to the "mainland" only via the waters of Lake Ladoga, and literally everything needed to stay alive (energy, fuel, provisions, military equipment, and troops) entered the city over the Road of Life, either by water or by ice or over the bottom of Ladoga. Thanks to this alone, the city withstood the blockade, and it was due to a great extent to the divers that this link with the rest of the country saved the city and its inhabitants from annihilation (Fig. 046).

The Volga: The Water Route

The Volga during the war, and even more so during the period of the Battle of Stalingrad, was an extremely important water route for the country, and divers played no small role here too in maintaining it in good working order.

Like the Road of Life on Lake Ladoga, the Volga was under enemy air strikes over its considerable length, both downstream of Stalingrad and upstream, and the emergency-rescue component in the overall bulk of diving work on the Volga was present in full measure. However, in contrast to the Road of Life on Lake Ladoga, the infrastructure for the Volga water route already existed, it was hardly necessary to build it anew, and the bulk of hydraulic-engineering work was limited to just rebuilding objects destroyed by bombing.

Several tasks lay before the divers on the Volga water route: searching for and eliminating non-contact bottom mines that were not amenable to minesweeping, raising military cargo from sunken vessels, salvaging vessels that could be restored and put into service, and clearing the waterways of sunken vessels that were navigational hazards and could not be restored.

The mine war that the Germans unfurled on the Volga in the summer of 1942, was a new thing for rivermen. Up to then, only the

Fig. 046: Preparing a diver to descend into the waters of the port of Kobon, on the "Road of Life," 1942. (Exhibit at the "Road of Life" Museum, settlement of Osinovets)

navy had been involved with non-contact bottom mines with a timer mechanism (which was described in the section on Mine Warfare). Only after repeated explosions in the waters of the Volga and both passenger and cargo ships blowing up, as well as large-tonnage water scows with troops and military cargo, was this problem given serious attention.

The first of such mines were found in the waterways along the lower reaches of the Volga, and, based on the description of divers, who were aided by fleet minemen, they were recognized as bottom mines with combination acoustic and magnetic fuses. After the mines were identified, it was clear how to deal with them.

The river was one of the main transportation arteries feeding Stalingrad. Ships and barges carried thousands of tons of cargo at a time, and every such vessel sunk by the enemy inflicted serious damage on army equipment. Precisely for this reason, then, the Front Command set the riverine rescue-service boatmen the main task of salvaging from sunken vessels the arms, ammunition, equipment, and various materiel needed on the front lines.

In the summer of 1942, in connection with the rapidly escalating volume of diving work and, even more so, of such specific operations as emergency-rescue work, the Riverine Fleet Narkomat had to create, practically from scratch, ship-salvage-and-rescue and military-construction detachments, for whom divers and diving equipment had to be gathered from all the technical sections of the water route, along with their wooden, floating, snag-lifting cranes. But problems arose with the divers. The war was already in its second year, and many divers had gone to the front. Even mobilizing cadets from the Training Detachment of the Ship-Salvage-and-Diving Service in the city of Vyaznik for work on the inland waterways, the situation was not saved, and young women who had graduated from light-diving courses at the OSVOD Union before the war had to be mobilized for the diving operations.

In order to increase the efficiency of unloading sunken vessels, the ship-salvage-and-rescue detachments were split up into diving groups. Each group was based at a wooden floating crane from a dive station, with a manual air pump on board. There were no telephone communications with the diver.

This is how one of the divers, Il'ya Petrovich Fomin, remembered unloading a sunken ship at that time, at a meeting with veterans in 1972:

> We worked three days, with interruptions, because a diver often had to surface when aircraft appeared. The Fascist vultures did not let even one man even slip by: they shelled and bombed. In the daytime on August 8, 1942, seventeen Heinkels bombed us again. One of them turned back and dropped three bombs on us. Luckily, the bombs flew past us and fell in the water. That rolled us smartly into the water and dirt and deafened us for a time. It wasn't deep in the backwater, but the deck of the barge went under. The divers strapped up crate after crate, Red Army soldiers dragged the crates manually onto a pontoon boat, sent them over to shore, and camouflaged them there. More than 5,000 crates with mines, over 100 heavy machine guns, and nearly a hundred field binoculars were lifted up from underneath the water and turned over to the front.

Diving work on the objects went on around the clock at first, but when the frequency of air attacks increased, they had to work at night.

Army units rendered substantial assistance to the ship-salvage-and-rescue groups. Two or three dozen Red Army soldiers were attached to each dive group, as needed, to handle the salvaged cargo, break it apart, dry it, and so on, and to perform ancillary work. And the work to break apart and dry the loads was no small one. In the period from August 3–25, 1942, for instance, a group of nine divers and more than 300 soldiers attached to them unloaded a barge sunk in the bombing. The uniforms brought up to the surface from its holds, broken apart, and dried out, made up 130 truckloads.

And such instances may be considered to be in the majority. In one year, from August 1942 to July 20, 1943, divers unloaded fifty-one sunken vessels, just on the Volga. From their holds, the following were salvaged and sent to the front or to defense plants: six aircraft, seven tanks, thirty-four motor vehicles, 33.9 thousand shells, 17,000 machine guns, 1.6 thousand tons of various types of weapon, 3.8 thousand tons of ammunition, 2.8 thousand tons of engineering equipment, 5.4 thousand tons of uniforms, 0.4 thousand tons of provisions and fodder, a large amount of ferrous and non-ferrous metals, rubber, and other cargo, and 40.4 thousand tons of oil products pumped off the sunken vessels.

Fig. 047: Graduation certificate for I. Rassimovich in November 1941 from the OSVOD diving courses, qualifying her as a light-diving instructor.

As we have already said, young women who had graduated from the OSVOD Union diving courses occupied a significant place in diving operations on the Volga. Some of them managed to seek out V.P. Kozlov, a diving specialist from the Podvodrechstroy.

Irina Rassimovich (recounted in 1994):

> It's funny for me to recall now that I was a diver once, a bold, brave girl, a sportswoman, and a Komsomol secretary. They didn't pack me off to the front.
>
> I graduated from the courses in May of 1941, and in October I was ordered to the city of Gorodets to the light-diving instructor's course of the USSR's OSVOD Union. In March 1942, I was assigned as a diving instructor for the Gorkiy city council. A large group of light divers for Gorkiy Oblast managed to be sent out to Stalingrad.
>
> Once, a diver was summoned for a ship in the Volga Military Flotilla in Gorkiy. The head of the Gorkiy OSVOD, Arkhipov, took me with him to that ship. The crew was shocked; they were

astonished to see a female diver. At that time, women were not allowed to step onto the deck of a ship. Arkhipov prevailed on the commander and started to get me ready to dive. They pointed out for me parts of an antiaircraft gun in the water. I searched on the bottom for the parts for a long time, down to my last gulp of air. I found more than they expected, and I brought them up. The thunder of applause broke out on the ship. Arkhipov always trusted me. That was not my first dive with him. I was calm and consistent; he really sensed my every step. They prepared a reward for me: a hot bath with soap and a good dinner. All that was a great piece of luck at that time.

Anya Gal'tseva (recounted in 1983):

I was born in 1922. The war found me in Moscow. At that time I was already a light diver. Since things were not taking shape very well at the front in 1942, especially on the Volga, I was sent in the autumn of that year just outside Stalingrad. I got into the 2nd Detachment of the Ship-Salvage-and-Rescue Service as a diver on October 22, 1942, and I was there until June 1, 1943, that is, until the detachment was transferred from the Riverine Fleet authorities to the Volga Riverine Flotilla.

Our group was alternately at Kamyshin, then in Gornyy Balykleya, and even in Saratov. Vessels and people were lost in all those places, like in Stalingrad itself. I often had to help out the ships in the 2nd Minesweeper Brigade of the Volga Flotilla. The minesweepers crept in the shallows, searching for enemy mines. Wire, bark fibers from sunken wood, steel lines, and fiber rope often got wound up on the screws and shafts. There were not enough divers in the flotilla. So we had to perform their functions on the ships too.

Besides knowing how to dive, you required a lot of physical strength too. To unwind wire wound on the shaft or screw like thread took two or more hours. But unless your reserve of compressed air and oxygen was empty, you were constantly in the water. I only worked with IPA type apparatus; I didn't dive with ventilated equipment. My colleagues, the guy divers, simply took care me. But we lived like friends, like one family. And I still remember: how it wasn't so tough with the cadres (the medical ones too), on the Volga; every ship-salvage-and-rescue group had its own medical worker, a paramedic. Usually a woman, with the rank of lieutenant. We were young then, our tasks seemed OK, and we didn't complain about how hard it was.

We worked, and the time flew by. We got up when the sun rose, we went to bed when it got dark. I worked with divers I. Ivanov and A. Timfeyev. I don't remember the others now.

The Northern Gateway for Lend-Lease Supplies

The salvage of sunken military cargo was of particularly great importance in the north, in the Murmansk region and along the shores of Kola Gulf and the Barents Sea. It was there that the sinking transports from Allied convoys, damaged by the Germans, tried to get to. Tanks, aircraft, weapons, ammunition, and other military cargo sent to us by the Allies on the Lend-Lease program also went down along with the transports. Divers in the Northern Fleet raised everything, to the best of their ability, from the sunken vessels, everything that might be of value to the country and the army. These loads numbered not in the dozens or hundreds but many thousands of tons, and they all passed through the hands of divers when they were lifted from beneath the waves.

Award citations follow, but now for the divers of the Northern Fleet.

Chief Petty Officer Vasiliy Alekseyevich Bezruchko, Diver 1st Class, 78th Northern Fleet, ASO NF: "For outstanding leadership and performance in complex diving tasks, resulting in 1,000 tons of the most valuable military equipment and cargo being recovered for the Homeland."

Diver 2nd Class Dmitriy Grigor'yevich Grigor'yev, commander of the diving section, 78th Detachment, ASO NF: "He personally salvaged more than 200 tons of valuable cargo and military equipment from sunken transports, including about 100 tons of ammunition."

Diver 3rd Class Dmitriy Grigor'yevich Kalinko, MVB-1, ASO NF: "Just in operations salvaging cargo from the sunken steamship *Steel Worker* ... he personally spent about 4,000 hours underwater and raised more than 400 tons of very valuable cargo and military equipment."

Petty Officer Andrey Pavlovich Dryakhlov, 2nd class diving petty officer, MVB-1 Dive Section, ASO NF: "He personally salvaged more than 300 tons of valuable military gear and equipment, including six medium tanks."

Chief Petty Officer Stepan Ivanovich Khromov, petty officer in Diving Group, 78th Detachment, ASO NF: "The dive post under his personal leadership lifted from the water and saved more than 1,000 tons of valuable military gear, including 200 tons of ammunition, explosives, and three medium tanks."

Diver 1st Class Sergey Petrovich Miroshnichenko, acting diving command petty officer, MBV-3: "He personally raised, under difficult conditions, from damaged and sunken transports, more than 300 tons of very valuable cargo and military equipment, including four medium tanks."

The history of salvaging American tanks is rather typical. At the beginning of 1942, the Germans sank the transport *Steel Worker*, which was not armored, as well as aircraft and other equipment, at the approaches to Murmansk. The ship sank in a depth of about 40 m. In the beginning of 1943, Northern Fleet divers brought to the surface twelve General Lee tanks [*Editor*: American M3 Lee tanks]. Specialists from a repair battalion "resuscitated" eleven vehicles, having already sent a twelfth one for spare parts. The restored tanks then took part in battles on the Karelian front.

Motor vehicles, tractors, and other military equipment lifted from under the water were restored in roughly the same way. But that was only a small part of what the divers found, strapped in, and readied for lift. Divers lifted out of the holds of sunken vessels various equipment, materials, metal, products, and other things. Diving operations were conducted both in the daylight and in the polar night, in calm and in gale, not just in the Black and Baltic Seas but beyond the Arctic Circle as well, in the Barents Sea.

Disarming and Raising Sunken Ships

An integral part of the diving operations in the war was ship salvage, including the disassembly of weapons from ships sunk as well as the repair of ships and vessels afloat, without docking. It's not possible to tell about all of these operations. Not only are they not supported by documentation, but they have simply disappeared from the record. But we shall try to shed light on the most typical examples in each group of missions, even so.

It must be said that raising a ship, in and of itself, is a protracted operation that's not done in a day or even a week, and, as a rule, ships in a ship-salvage formation, once they have taken up their position over a vessel to be raised, cannot be arbitrarily moved to hide from enemy fire. There's practically nowhere for them to hide; at sea, they are like sitting ducks. So ships were raised either in case of extreme need, as was done with the sunken U-250 (more about this later; it was raised with hardly any loss, thanks to the fact that Finland, whose shore batteries were firing while the Soviets were operating in the area, left the war and were no longer a hindrance to salvaging), or else in those cases when it was possible to work at night but daytime operations had ceased, as was the case with raising an armed gunboat at Stalingrad (and about this too, a little later).

Raising Ammunition and Disassembling Weapons

In those cases when it was impossible to raise a sunken ship due either to its severe damage, the absence of ship-salvage resources, or to enemy opposition, we were limited to disassembly of the weapons and removal of the ammunition from the sunken ship, even more so if in the short time it had been underwater both guns and ammunition were still fully capable of use; they could be set down at shore batteries and go into operation.

Lifting ammunition from ships and transports sunk by the enemy, including barges, was quite a widespread diving operation. It was even more important that the brief time the ammunition stayed underwater did not, as a rule, affect its usefulness, and once raised to the surface, it could be used for its intended purpose.

Such operations were conducted in all the water basins where combat actions were being conducted.

An example of such an operation might be KBF divers raising mines from a barge sunk at Oranienbaum. Let us turn once more to excerpts from award citations:

> Petty Officer V.M. Petrenko, working in the complement of a dive station on unloading ammunition from barge No.5248 in Oranienbaum Military Port in the month of September 1943, demonstrated superior diving skills, dexterity, and fearlessness in working with such an unusual cargo. In spite of the clear danger of the explosion of mines being dropped all around the barge (due to poor visibility at the operational site), Comrade Petrenko unloaded, by hand with his dive buddy, in the course of six days from a depth of 29.5 feet, 4,500 152 mm shells and mines, thereby carrying out the urgent mission to save such a large quantity of ammunition.

A similar operation was the salvage in the Volga of the already mentioned 2,720 crates of shells for Katyusha rocket launchers from on-board a sunken barge.

In the Black Sea, ammunition was raised from on-board sunken ships along with artillery weapons.

But the ammunition on board the ships was not always harmless. In preparing to salvage a destroyer from the Northern Fleet, a spontaneous explosion of two deep bombs occurred, which were

Fig. 048: Raising the gun turret from the gunboat *Olekma* on the "Road of Life" on Lake Ladoga in 1943(?).

on board the ship. As a result of the explosion, the divers, M. Shimbarov and I. Pristenskiy, who were working underwater at that moment, were killed.

Disassembly of weapons, particularly at shallow depths, could be carried out with few resources and using auxiliary means, as was done on the Road of Life, for instance (Fig. 048).

Disassembly of the artillery from large ships by auxiliary means was more complicated to execute, but divers mastered and performed even this operation quite successfully, especially if the lost ship was at the moorage at the time it sank and was at a shallow depth, as was the case, for instance, with removing ammunition from the destroyer-leader *Tashkent* at Novorossiysk or the destroyer *Sovershennyy* at Sevastopol.

There was no problem with the destroyer-leader *Tashkent*, sunk at Novorossiysk in 1942. The deck of the ship, lying at the bottom of the moorage, was practically at sea level. Artillery and torpedo devices were removed from the ship, along with rangefinder and navigation equipment. It was proposed to use the destroyer-leader's guns for the defense of Novorossiysk, including putting

Fig. 049: The 130 mm gun from the destroyer *Sovershennyy [Perfect]* at the battery on Malakhov Hill.

one 130 mm gun on the destroyer *Besploshchadnyy* [*Ruthless*], and sending a 76 mm antiaircraft system to the lead Project-30 destroyer *Ognevoy* [*Militant*], which was under construction.

Roughly the same history befell the destroyer *Sovershennyy* in Sevastopol.

On September 30, 1941, the *Sovershennyy* was blown up by a mine near Sevastopol and was heavily damaged. Rescuers, together with the crew of the sinking ship, were able to drag it to a shallow spot in Kazach'ya Bay, where it lay on the bottom. On 1 October, using two eighty-five-ton ship-salvage pontoons, the damaged ship was towed into Sevastopol and put into a floating dock. But even in the midst of the docking process, bombing began, and the *Sovershennyy* received additional damage to the hull and sank again, along with a large crane, but this time right at the dock. Its large-caliber guns were ripped off by bomb explosions and tossed onto the deck of the dock. Over the next two days, under bombardment and artillery fire (these were the days of the first assault on Sevastopol), the salvagers raised the guns, and they were set up at the battery at Malakhov Hill (Fig. 049).

Ship Salvage

In those cases when they attempted to raise a rather large ship in an enemy action zone, even one lying at a moorage at a depth of several meters, the matter usually ended with large losses for the salvagers, and the salvage itself did not end in success, as was the case with the destroyer-leader *Tashkent* at Novorossiysk.

We said earlier that ship salvage in areas subject to bombardment, and even more so to artillery fire in the waters the enemy was watching, was an exception, and not many such salvages were successful. We shall present, as an example, just a few of them on the Volga and under maritime conditions.

At the beginning of October 1942 in Stalingrad, in the area of the tractor factory, the armored gunboat BK-32 was damaged, and it sank, unable to reach the opposite shore of the Volga. The shore was thoroughly shelled by the Germans with mortars and artillery, but the command authorities could not come to terms with the loss of such a powerful combat unit as an armored boat. The gunboat had to be raised.

Under of direct line-of-sight and fire from the enemy, it was impossible to salvage the boat by traditional methods, using flotation means and pontoons, and the work had to be done in secret from the shore. At night, a camouflaged work area was cleared in the bushes, diving gear was placed there, and nighttime dives were organized. It was a long way to the boat from the dive site, and in order to reach it, hoses from two dive stations had to be linked together into a single line. A diver, working in ventilated equipment, inspected the armored boat and found in its hull numerous holes from shells. It was not possible to seal the hull after patching the holes and closing all the on-deck hatches, and it was decided to "float" the boat using soft ship-salvage pontoons. Divers hung the pontoons in the boat compartments, attached them to a dive pump, and set up a winch on shore. Before inflating the pontoons, our artillery opened fire on the German positions, the pontoons were inflated "on the sly," the boat floated, they dragged it to shore with the winch and camouflaged in the bushes. Later, the salvaged boat was towed by other armored gunboats to a safe place on the Akhtuba River, and there it was dragged ashore and repaired. The saved armored boat fought on the Volga up to the end of the Battle of Stalingrad, and then it was deployed on the Dnepr near Kiev.

But even on the Volga, where depths were not great, the shore covered with shrubbery offered definite cover, the distances to the object allowed ventilated equipment to be used, and the very vessels being salvaged had a comparatively low displacement, the task of

Fig. 050: The armored gunboat BK-32, half-submerged as a result of enemy fire. Put out of action by the enemy, ships often managed to reach shore and sank in the nearshore zone or the shallows. Because of this, divers, working secretly from shore, could "float" the sunken boats in order to tow them to the rear later for repairs. (Photo: 1942, Stalingrad, from the TsVMM collections)

raising a vessel under enemy eyes was extremely difficult. In port or at sea, on the open water, in direct view of the enemy, it was incomparably more difficult. And this related to ship salvage on the Baltic and in the Black Sea.

It must be said that, based on the level of problems for the divers, the enemy artillery shelling was worse than the bombing. If it was possible to anticipate an expected bombardment in advance, allowing time for a diver to surface, even if the decompression procedure was violated, you only knew about artillery fire with the explosion of the first shells. But for a diver on the bottom, the explosion of a shell under water, even a decent distance away, was like dying, due to the hydraulic shock caused by the explosion.

On the whole, however, from the diver's point of view, ship salvage in the first years of the war was not especially complicated, insofar as ship salvage was an uncomplicated operation. The depths were not great, the operation sites were, as a rule, secure from wave action like (the waters of ship-repair facilities and naval bases, whether Sevastopol, Leningrad, or Novorossiysk), but enemy action, bombing, or artillery shelling often made this work flat-out dangerous or simply impossible.

The command authorities highly valued the dedication of the divers who worked underwater and under enemy fire, and this was noted as an essential fact in divers' award citations. As an example, note the award citation for Petty Officer Nikolay Moiseyevich Litvinov, section commander, Ship-Salvage Detachment, EPRON Rescue Section, KBF:

> Comrade Litvinov, working from September 7 through December 1, 1943, on salvaging the frigate Pioneer, demonstrated the best models of valor, courage, and merit in labor.
>
> Working under difficult conditions associated with enemy proximity, when the latter was lighting up the work area with star shells and spotlights as well as shelling the work area with fougasse shells, Comrade Litvinov, underwater every 5 hours as the first of the dive complement, went over the arrangements and, with exceptional efficacy, gained huge successes throughout a most labor-intensive diving operation, flushing out tunnels and trenches, thereby shortening the time to accomplish the work.
>
> While working at the docks at the Kanonerskiy plant in the spring of this year, the work site was literally strewn with shells in a sudden attack of enemy fire. Comrade Litvinov, being at that moment underwater, was deafened by the explosion. The personnel who were at the pumps were tossed aside by the explosion and Litvinov was without air for some time. Due only to his composure, he got his bearings quickly under hazardous conditions, and his personal courage allowed Comrade Litvinov to exit the water. After some time, having physically recovered, he returned to the water again.
>
> For demonstrated courage, valor, and heroism in labor while salvaging the frigate Pioneer, in direct proximity to the enemy, I recommend that Petty Officer N.M. Litvinov be awarded the State decoration of the Order of the Great Patriotic War, 1st Degree.

Here is a second case from a whole series of similar ones that arose when dive stations were shelled. One time, on Ladoga on the Road of Life during an artillery attack, a shell fragment struck one of the cylinders on the manual dive pump, and the pump jammed. At that time, a diver, Aleksandr Bartusenko, was down below. As described in his award citation: "... being without air, he did not lose courage and, stopping the air exhausting from his diving dress, he succeeded in exiting the water unharmed."

But let us return to ship salvage. We must particularly note the differences between ship-salvage operations in the initial period of the war and those carried out at its end. In the beginning of the war, we were boxed in on our naval bases, and the enemy could reach virtually every point, if not with artillery fire, then by bombing. At the end of the war, the front had rolled off to the west, leaving behind hundreds and thousands of sunken vessels, but ... this was already the deep rear, and it was humanly possible to work there without risking receiving a shell at your feet or a bomb on your head. And from the point of view of the safety of underwater operations, this was hardly a defining moment.

But still one to remember. When conducting diving sabotage and recon operations, a commando diver fulfills his mission independently from the beginning until the end result is achieved: sabotaging or delivering information to command authorities in the complete absence of any minimal support provided from the surface. When salvaging sunken military cargos, support from the surface was also comparatively minor, generally rigging operations (not taking into account the organization of the dive itself). When carrying out ship-salvage work, the role of the diver is purely secondary: to inspect, cut off or fasten a line or a strap, etc., while dozens of the most varied specialists on the surface perform the major work of the salvage. But the diver's work, because of it, does not make it easier or less dangerous; his share in the overall volume of work simply changes.

Let's give several of the most typical examples of ship salvage carried out at sea in the first years of the war.

Raising a ship in the waters of a naval base. On September 21, 1941, during a massed attack of enemy aircraft on Kronstadt, two 50 kg bombs fell on the stern of the destroyer-leader *Minsk*: one tore into the superstructure; the second, going through the deck, lodged inside the hull. One more bomb exploded in the water beside the ship in the area of the boiler room and damaged a boiler. It began to take on water, the destroyer was left without power, and it drifted toward the shore and, listing 8°, settled by the stern on the bottom. After the end of the attack, a patch was placed over the largest holes, and they partially pumped out the water and towed the *Minsk*, without power, to the south wall of Kronstadt Military Harbor.

But the bombings continued. As a result, the ship received additional damage and, the moorings having torn apart, it sank a distance of sixteen feet from the wall in a depth of twenty-eight feet and listing forty degrees to port.

An inspection of the ship showed that it could be raised, restored, and put back in service.

Salvage operations began in the middle of October 1941 under the leadership of Senior Lieutenant G.P. Titov and continued until the harbor froze. It was decided to turn the *Minsk*, which had a displacement of 300 tons, onto an even keel on the bottom, using six pairs of seventy-ton tackles and two eighty-ton and one forty-ton pontoons, and then to patch the most serious holes, pump out the water, set it afloat, and tow it to a dock for hull repair.

Fig. 051: Raising the destroyer-leader *Minsk* in Kronstadt Military Harbor, 1942.

The salvage operations began with the removal of ammunition from the ship. Then, after the winter, all the necessary preparations were accomplished, and toward August, in spite of constant shelling and bombardment, which dealt more and more new damage to the ship, everything was ready to lift it (Fig. 051).

On August 19, the final pump-out from the hull of the *Minsk* was done, the ship floated up, and it was towed to a dock at the Kronstadt Naval Plant.

The attempt to raise the destroyer-leader *Tashkent* at Novorossiysk was less successful.

The *Tashkent* (built in 1939, with a displacement of more than 4,000 tons, a length of about 459 feet, and a crew of about 350) was in the Black Sea Fleet and had been providing support to besieged Sevastopol, delivering to the city guns, ammunition, provisions, and replenishment and evacuating the wounded and civilian populace. On one trip, the *Tashkent* fell under bombardment, was damaged, and headed for Novorossiysk with the assistance of emergency rescue forces in the Black Sea Fleet.

But on July 2, 1942, in the middle of the day and standing at the Elevator moorage in Novorossiysk, the damaged ship suffered a new bombing strike by more than three-dozen German bombers. The *Tashkent* received two direct hits and lay on the bottom (Fig. 052).

Fig. 052: The destroyer-leader *Tashkent* at Elevator mooring, port of Novorossiysk, after a bombing, July 2, 1942.

Of the 344 men on board, seventy-six died and seventy-seven were wounded.

On July 19, 1942, the Military Council of the Black Sea Fleet gave the order to raise the ship by August 15, 1942, but this turned out to be not quite so simple. Novorossiysk was in an area that was accessible to enemy aviation, and any activity on board the *Tashkent* resulted in bombardment. While attempts were being made to raise the ship, the enemy sank three dive boats and a heavy-lift ship with their two on-board dive stations, as well as four 1,000 t/hr-capacity motorized pumps.

In the end, the endeavors to raise the *Tashkent* under enemy fire failed, and the ship was raised only in 1944 after the liberation of Novorossiysk. After the salvage, it was discovered that the ship's hull had widespread damage. It was not expedient to restore the *Tashkent*, and the destroyer was scrapped for its metal.

One more example: a ship salvage within the bounds of a naval base. The heavy cruiser *Petropavlovsk* with a displacement of 15,900 tons was purchased from Germany in unfinished condition and in May of 1940, it was towed to Leningrad. At the beginning of the war, there were already two large-caliber, double-gun turrets on the cruiser, as well as small-caliber antiaircraft artillery. As the Germans approached Leningrad, the uncompleted cruiser, which had no power of its own yet, supported our troops with gunfire from its eight-inch guns. On the morning of September 17, 1941, the Germans got back at the ship that had been annoying them, and they shelled it point-blank. That day, the cruiser took fifty-three 210 mm shells. As a result, the ship developed numerous holes in the hull, some of which covered an area of up to ninety-eight square feet, and a fire broke out, caused by explosions in the internal spaces. The ship began to list to port. To prevent it from capsizing, the seacocks were opened and the cruiser settled without a list onto the bottom in a depth of twenty-six feet, in direct view of the enemy. A special group of Germans was watching the ship with great interest, preparing at any moment to disrupt any salvage operations.

The value of the cruiser to our command, with its great firepower, was obvious, and it was decided to raise the cruiser. The lift plan anticipated patching the holes and floating the ship by pumping the water out of its hull. All this in plain view of the enemy, under precision fire.

Work on raising the ship began at the end of November 1941, and continued for 180 workdays, with a break for the winter. The divers and riggers, under the leadership of Engineer Lieutenant-Captain A.P. Tsekhmistro, worked at night in complete darkness (for the cruiser lift, you may recall, was being done in full view of the enemy). Drying the compartments one after the other, they managed to float the ship. As the water was pumped out with the suction pumps and its level reduced in the compartments, openings in the bulkheads were hermetically sealed with patches, chocks, and oakum, the piping was uncoupled in the dried-out compartments, and plugs were driven in. During trial pumping, the ship repeatedly rose up, but toward morning, in order to keep the work hidden from view, they flooded it again and set it on the bottom.

Finally, the preparations for floating the ship were finished. On the night of September 17, 1942, the salvagers performed the final pumping, the cruiser was afloat, the tugs *Iceberg* and *K-1* literally brought it out from under the enemy's nose and delivered it to the wall of the Baltic plant. As was discovered later, the commander of the German unit, in whose view the cruiser had been rendered "inoperable," was shot for this.

In January 1944, while executing operations throughout the fascist rout near Leningrad, the *Petropavlovsk*, as part of a long-range naval-artillery group, destroyed permanent enemy fortifications, communications, military equipment, and infantry concentrations. The cruiser launched more than a thousand heavy shells against

German-Finnish positions, shells, it so happens, of German manufacture.

One more example: raising a submarine in the open ocean.

The story of searching for and salvaging the German U-250 is somewhat off the beaten track and is interesting for a number of reasons. First of all, this is a rare instance of a classic ship salvage, carried out in an area in clear view of the enemy and during active counterattacks. Secondly, as a result of the above, this is an example of every variant of the effect of artillery fire and bombardment during the conduct of diving operations, as well as of the effects on the diver himself under the water. And finally, this story is a professional description, related by a physician and special physiologist, Vladimir Ivanovich Tyurinyy, who participated World War II and who knew the principal executors of the operations personally, having served many years with I.V. Prokhvatilov after the war and who had the information first-hand.

Thus, in July 1944, a small naval subhunter, MO-103, attacked the German U-250, which was submerged. Under the jolts from depth charges, the boat sank, and only six total of its crew were saved, including the boat commander. Upon interrogation, the commander revealed that torpedoes of a new construction type were on board and they were set to explode in the event the U-boat was captured.

This information was indirectly confirmed by the fact that Germans showed activity unusual for such situations with sunken U-boats, covering the site of the boat's loss with artillery fire (it was lost in an active zone of Finnish shore artillery) and ship bombardment, which was taking place in this area.

After a report to Admiral V.F. Tributs, the KBF commander, on all the circumstances associated with the U-250, a decision was made to post a guard in the area where the boat had sunk and to raise it "at all costs."

They set a round-the-clock watch, and it was not in vain. The Germans repeatedly tried to bomb the boat using torpedo boats with depth charges, but their boats could not break through the barrier of Baltic fleet ships.

At the same time, Specops Company, Recon Section, KBF Command was ordered to find the boat, inspect it, and remove documents from it: charts, code books, and so forth. For this purpose, a special group was put together from the company complement and which went out to the place where the boat had sunk on a tender (a so-called self-propelled pontoon boat) (Fig. 053) and accompanied by the small subhunter MO-103.

Fig. 53: Blockade tender (a self-propelled pontoon bridge) that Leningrad workshops produced during the blockade. Such tenders were widely used as auxiliary flotation means, including on the "Road of Life" and at the Nevskaya Dubrovka crossing.

The task set by the command for the group, commanded by I.V. Prokhvatilov, the RON commander, was, from the diving viewpoint, far from simple.

First of all, the coordinates indicated for the place where the boat had sunk were not accurate. In the heat of battle, the subhunter crew that had dropped depth charges on the boat was not sure where it was, and the U-boat commander also knew his approximate position, in general, but a buoy that the subhunter had set at the place where the boat went down was sabotaged. On the other hand, hydroacoustic search means, if you could call them that, were more than a little primitive in 1944, and it was forbidden to rely on them either. To top it all off, the suits used by RON divers were not suitable for swimming in the blue. In those years, our recon divers could not swim at all underwater; they only walked along the bottom, with all the problems resulting from that.

Secondly, the boat lay at a depth of more than ninety-eight feet, and the RON divers directing their search were using VIA-2 apparatus with closed-circuit breathing (Fig. 054). With this apparatus, a diver breathed pure oxygen, but at depths over sixty-five, the oxygen acted on the central nervous system like a strong poison, causing cramps and loss of consciousness. At a depth of 98–115 feet, that is, at the depth at which the U-boat lay, oxygen poisoning occurs after just eight minutes. In peacetime, walking along at such depths with oxygen was categorically prohibited.

They found the boat visually. They towed a diver behind the dive boat at a slow pace, and he simply looked around. In the words of the submariners who had been saved, the U-250 lay on the bottom with almost no list. The sea depth in the area of the search was about ninety-eight feet, and the U-boat itself was a little less than thirty-three feet tall. Thus, from a depth of 49–65 feet (and it was entirely possible for a diver to descend that far in oxygen breathing gear), it would be possible to see the boat in the comparatively clean-water conditions of the open sea.

True, it was only possible to search this way in daylight, under potential artillery fire and bombardment.

V.K. Vlasov, an RON physician and special physiologist, recalled later:

Fig. 054: Light diver during World War II. Soldiers in the RON used this type of equipment when searching for the U-250. These were Type E, "dry" suits (in the photograph) or Type TU-1 suits (Fig. 80) with a VIA-2 or IPA Series oxygen-breathing apparatus on the chest. (Photo from the collections of the Red Banner Baltic Fleet Museum, city of Baltiysk)

> We had sent the diver down, when suddenly a voice boomed out from the MO-103 over a megaphone: "Periscope starboard, prepare for deep depth charges!" We were not able to raise the diver, as the depth charges had already begun to drop. The distance (from the subhunter) was no more than a hundred meters. Violating every instruction on gradual ascents, as a group, we pulled energetically and as quickly as possible on the safety line, thinking: "Is our guy alive?" With great good fortune, he turned out to be alive and unharmed, but then it was Chief Nikitin, an light-diving instructor. Coming up on deck, he swore heartily (to put it mildly), not understanding the reason for his sudden and superfast ascent. He had barely managed to bleed down the air from his breathing bag, but experience had managed to help him to do it.
>
> This event remains unclear to me to this day. How could a light diver, upon ascending from a depth of sixty-five feet, remain uninjured when deep charges were being tearing by at a hundred meters and our boat was being tossed around like a seashell?

Vlasov further recalled:

> The search went on. Toward the end of the fourth day, the sea was covered with a rare layer of Baltic herring (due to the deep depth charges) and with large spots of fuel oil (from sunken

boats) ... Almost the entire search group was gathered on the fore-deck, headed up by Prokhvatilov; they decided how to make a further attempt, and reported to fleet headquarters.

And suddenly we saw a patch of air bubbles on the surface of a layer of salt-water fish, and we all burst out as one: "The U-boat! Stop the engine!" After that, the following happened: Chief Nikitin quickly donned his mask (we had all remained in our diving dress and apparatus) and rapidly departed under the water. Diver Fadeyev, who had just finished his time underwater and was already taking his mask off, hearing the shout of "U-boat!," quickly put his mask back on and in an instant dropped into the water. A third diver, getting ready to relieve Fadeyev, also dropped precipitously into the water. And after being down for some ten minutes, we brought Nikitin back up, based on signals on the safety lines, with blood streaming from his ears, along with Fadeyev, with incipient signs of oxygen poisoning (tonic cramps). The third diver informed us that the U-boat was underneath us, but the depth turned out to be greater than ninety-eight feet. That meant it would only be possible to work for a limited amount of time.

The commander made the decision to utilize ventilated gear, the more so since it had telephone communications. Petty Officer Gupalov went down and after several minutes we heard his voice: "I'm standing at the U-boat conning tower." They then determined the precise depth: it turned out to be 118 feet, an unusual depth for the Gulf of Finland. Since darkness had fallen, they were forced to cut short the work until morning. Having strapped down various floating objects with ropes, they could determine that way where the U-boat lay. The commander reported the successful search results to fleet headquarters. At dawn, they were on-site once again.

Since one of the divers had been oxygen-poisoned at depth, Vlasov decided to check himself whether it was possible to exceed the authorized instructions, to spend only eight minutes at this depth. Really, it would be impossible for sure in that length of time to even inspect the object, to say nothing of finding your way into the boat's compartments and locating anything there.

Vlasov recollected:

So, in light diving dress, the summer model (with no gloves) and a VIA-2 apparatus, I dropped down to the hull of the U-boat, stood on deck at the conning tower, and went through an open

> hatch into the inner hull, but the complete darkness offered no possibility of determining anything by sight.
>
> By feel, some kind of metallic object fell into my hands, which I grabbed, and I started to climb out the conning tower, but some kind of line was being pulled behind this object (it turned out later it was a power cable, and the metal box turned out to be a distributing switchboard). I had to yank it in order to free the object.
>
> At that moment, I felt the first symptoms of oxygen toxicity (a sudden twitching in the eyelids), I gave the signal to lift me up, and suddenly tonic cramps occurred in my hands, not allowing me to move them at all or hold onto the signal line. Luckily for me, at that very moment, our diver, Sergey Nepomnyashchiy, had begin to descend in ventilated diving dress, we met at the same level, and our safety lines happened to get wound together. He came up to me with his light and saw that the "doctor was smuggling some object to him with all his strength, but it looked unnatural somehow," and he gave the order by phone to lift both of us up together, which was quickly done. Coming on board, I saw the blue sky, they took metal object out of my hands, and I lost consciousness. I came to in about five minutes, according to my colleagues, and I saw I was lying on deck, they had poured water over me from a bucket, and someone was trying to give me something to sniff. Seeing that I was coming to my senses, the commander breathed a sigh of relief and noted with his customary humor: "Well, doctor, we aren't going to let you go down any more, or who of us would save you?" I had spent twelve minutes underwater, exceeding the norm by a total of four minutes. The tables were accurate.

All the same, in order to increase the time for staying underwater just a little even, Vlasov resolved for the divers to perform not a triple but a single flush of the light-diving apparatus with oxygen before descending. As a result, when switching on breathing into the apparatus, nitrogen stayed in the breathing mixture, while the amount of oxygen in it was consequently reduced, its toxic action was lessened, and the diver could work at depth a little longer but, unfortunately, only a little longer.

One of the participants in the operation, I.A. Udalov, a RON diver, wrote later:

> We crept about all day on the bottom ... travelling by touch. After lying on deck a little and exhaling the toxic oxygen, we went back

> again and again into the water. No one, of course, managed more than eight minutes. Several times, they pulled Volodya Borisov, Seva Anan'yev, me, and many other divers out with clouded eyes and foaming at the mouth.
>
> The shelling began. A first shell flew past, a second one didn't reach us. The third shell would be ours. And it tore by very close indeed, throwing up a huge column of water and everyone who was on deck was rolled head over heels.

Nevertheless, in spite of all the problems with the shelling and artillery fire, they discovered that the U-boat was lying on a rocky bottom, its bow was resting on a rock ridge, and below the hull there was a free space (which made strapping on pontoons later considerably easier during the lift). There was a slight list to starboard, and no pitch. The conning-tower hatch was open (through which the crew members we saved had exited). On the port side in the area of the Diesel compartment, there was a large hole, through which the interior of a compartment was visible. It also became clear that to pass via the conning tower into the boat in oxygen gear, find the necessary documents, and return to our boat in ten minutes would be physically impossible. There remained the use of gear in which the diver breathed not oxygen but air, and at that depth he would have at least an hour of time to work. In those years, only ventilated equipment offered that opportunity.

Luckily, and it could be that this was due to the commander's intuition, although ordinarily recon divers used light-diving oxygen gear, there was a diving instructor for ventilated equipment in the company complement and he had instructed the divers. So the dive boat with the needed equipment dashed off to where the U-boat had sunk, and they dropped Sergey Nepomnyashchiy into the water. He was able to penetrate into the U-boat in an hour, get as far as the commander's and navigator's cabins, collect the charts into a special case, and return to the hatch where his comrades were waiting. But this did not happen without incident. Sergey then told, with a goodly amount of emotion, about his entry into the U-boat:

> I undogged the compartment, and out of it floated body after body. White, bloated ... They gaped toward me in the light. The lantern almost dropped out of my hands. But I endured it; I didn't pay attention to them. I went on through into the captain's and navigator's cabins, removed whatever there were of charts and took the case. I turned back, but the drowned men had collected at the ladder. They wanted to float up at will, to be

> drawn up to the surface. Evidently the current had caused that. I moved them aside and went to the ladder fast. But no such luck! Wait, I knew it! They were stuck behind the hoses, they were pressing against my shoulders. There were sparks in front of my eyes after all this ... and my legs were getting weak. I had apparently forgotten to bleed off the air in my fright: my suit was deflating. Well, it was a no-go! I've had it, I thought, and then I screamed bloody murder.

In the end, they retrieved the case with the charts, and thus the RON divers accomplished their mission to look for the U-boat and removed documents from it.

The command assessed the work of the RON divers highly. Several of the award citations are presented below for participants in the operation searching for the U-boat and confiscating documentation from it.

Capt. 3rd Rank Ivan Vasil'yevich Prokhvatilov, commander, Specops Company, KBF Reconnaissance Command: "In the beginning of August, he took an active part as leader ... in the search for a sunken enemy submarine. In spite of his own injury which had not healed and enemy artillery fire at the site where recon divers were searching for the submarine, the U-boat was found and further operations were assigned to the KBF ASO. For demonstrated skill and courage in leading the work of the divers in searching for a sunken enemy submarine, I request that Comrade Prokhvatilov be awarded the Order of the Red Star."

Senior Lt. Vladimir Kuz'mich Vlasov, Medical Diving Service, doctor of Specops Company, KBF Reconnaissance Command:

> In the beginning of August 1944, he took an active part in the search for an enemy submarine sunk in Vyborg Bay.
>
> In spite of artillery fire on the part of the enemy, the sunken U-boat was found and he was the first to penetrate into its interior, after which he led subsequent work on KBF ASO preparations to salvage it.
>
> For the excellent provision of medical and health measures to the operation's light divers and for his direct participation in the search operations, both searching and working on the enemy U-boat found, he is deserving of the State award of the Order of the Patriotic War, 2nd Degree.

Sergey Aleksandrovich Nepomnyashchiy, light recon diver, Specops Company, Recon Section, KBF Command:

He is an excellent light recon diver. He has taken part in reconnaissance and sabotage operations in which he demonstrated bravery and courage.

In July 1944, he actively participated in searches for booby-trap mines, and in the beginning of August 1944, under conditions of enemy artillery action, he took part in a search for a sunken enemy submarine, and after it was found, he carefully inspected the submarine for the purpose of raising it. For tenacity and courage demonstrated in operations conducted, which provided the command with valuable information concerning the enemy, and for successfully accomplishing tasks in the search and inspecting an enemy U-boat under artillery fire, I request that he be awarded the Order of the Red Star.

Vladimir Ivanovich Zaytsev, light commando-diver, Specops Company, Recon Section, KBF Command: "... in the beginning of August 1944, he took an active part in the search for a sunken enemy submarine, and after its discovery he inspected the U-boat for the purpose of raising it. For demonstrated tenacity and courage in the operations conducted and for the successful accomplishment of the search and inspection mission for the enemy U-boat under artillery fire, I request that he be awarded the Order of the Patriotic War 2nd Degree."

Raising the submarine was assigned to the emergency rescue service of the Baltic Fleet. Several dive boats were engaged for the lift, three tugs, a tender, and later, the rescue vessels *Tsitsilia* [*Cecilia*] and *Sirena* [*Siren*] from the KBF's 76th ASO. The work was done at night, since the Finnish shore artillery was shelling the work area from dawn on.

It was decided to lift the U-boat, which had a displacement of about 700 tons, by the classic method, using 200-ton, steel, ship-salvage pontoons. Luckily, tunnels did not have to be flushed out to pass the ship-salvage straps underneath the hull. The bow strap was hooked through a clear space between the hull and the bottom, and the stern strap was hung under the stern overhang in the "screw window." The hooked straps were fastened to two 200-ton, ship-salvage pontoons, which they then easily inflated so that they were afloat.

The work went on under artillery fire and bombardment. More than once, the divers, who were under the water, suffered contusions and ear barotrauma, as well as decompression sickness when an emergency ascent was necessary. Few documents remain on the raising of the U-boat, and we turn again to the award citations for participants in this operation, which contain, if you will, the most objective description of episodes in this unique operation.

Sometimes when wave swells were high, a pontoon broke a diver's air hose, who at that instant was at a depth of ninety-two feet. The diver was ordered not to exhaust the air from his diving dress, and they brought him rapidly up to the surface in an emergency lift. They extracted the diver, who was already unconscious, from his diving dress. He had been rapidly poisoned by carbon dioxide gas that had accumulated in his helmet in the absence of ventilation. Award citations were found for an officer who had been on deck at the time of the emergency and for a diver who had been working on the submarine at that moment.

Lt. Aleksandr Dmitriyevich Razuvayev: "When the connection with the diver, Sirotkin, was severed, (the lieutenant) was the first to find that the manometer was showing a different pressure. He immediately understood that the air hose was broken, and he personally hauled the diver in, he found a hole in the hose right away, squeezed it, and saved Petty Officer Sirotkin."

Petty Officer Petr Vasil'yevich Sirotkin, diving petty officer: "He descended in scale 5 waves to a depth of 82–88 feet. The working conditions were exceptionally difficult, but he continued to work. The air hose and the phone line were put out of action. The danger of dying hung over the diver, but Sirotkin did not lose courage. Having been without air for more than a minute, as a result of adhering to proper protocol (by expelling the minimum amount of air), he did not die."

In a word, the case of the diver, Sirotkin, with his air hose broken by the pontoon, was not unique at all, but it happened that similar situations did not end so luckily. We said earlier that the conditions in time of war did not always allow the safety requirements for diving operations to be met. So, in the Northern Fleet while strapping in military cargo on-board the transport ship *Steel Worker* at a depth of 131 feet, the diver I. Frolov died due to a broken air hose.

Emergency ascents of divers working on U-boat U-250, led, as a result of shellings and bombardment, to five cases of divers' decompression sickness. The first times, the boats, which had no decompression chambers, went into hiding, the divers dropped under the water again, and they came up only in accordance with medical procedures. For instance, diver and senior Red Navy sailor Vasiliy Sergeyevich Sokur: "... worked twice at a depth of 65–88 feet for more than five hours. Due to the shelling and close proximity of falling shells, he was occasionally plucked out of the water without no delay. After a delay, he dove back down into the bay."

Something similar happened to Petty Officer Timofey Prokof'yevich Golenko, commander of the diving section: "He continued to work underwater, when at a distance of twelve to fifteen cables from the object (he was working on), a battle arose between our shore batteries and boats and the enemy's boats. He accomplished the task set in full. Because dawn was coming and because the situation was getting worse, he was taken out of the water without delay, upon which he was plunked into the bay."

And there were a lot of such cases.

Only with the arrival of the rescue ship *Sirena* at the work site, with a recompression chamber on board, did they begin to carry out medical recompression for the divers in the chamber in a "humane" manner. They placed a diver "in critical condition" in the chamber at the same pressure at which he had been underwater, they held the pressure there for ten minutes, and then proceeded to decompress normally.

In those cases when it was not possible to stop working at dawn, smokescreen boats were used (Fig. 055). Sometimes the cloud of smoke laid by the boats had a diameter of more than three kilometers and a height of about 1,640 feet. It had to be by guesswork for the enemy to shoot and drop bombs. The smoke was such that at times you couldn't see the stern from the bow of the ship. It made the sailors' eyes run, it tickled their throats, and what can you say about the divers, who were getting this half-smoky air pumped under the water. Even though you had filters, the filters could hardly purify it completely.

It must be noted that the enemy was not limited to just shelling and bombing in trying so hard to prevent the submarine from being raised. During the salvage operation, they made several attempts to destroy the U-boat with all of its on-board weapons and equipment, which were secret at that time, taking no particular care about their losses. Our aircraft, covering the work site, repeatedly disrupted the attempts of the Germans to drop bombs on the ship-salvage ship formation. But occasionally, when enemy torpedo boats tore through their guard, they were able to set out a mine barrier around the places they assumed the U-boat was and even dropped several dozen depth charges on it, hoping to destroy its hull and cause the torpedoes to detonate. But the boat was not harmed as a result of this attempt, while the Germans lost three boats in battling with the guard ships.

Thus, they set about work on August 10, by August 22, they had a bow pontoon strapped on, and in another four days, the stern one. On August 29, they began to inflate the pontoons. However, a sudden gale not only made it necessary to stop inflating, but it tore off the pontoons and tossed them ashore on one of the nearest islands, right in sight of the enemy artillery battery. But the Finns did not succeed in firing on them. Capt. 2nd Rank Anatoliy Seliverstovich Kurdin,

Fig. 055: Laying down a smokescreen from on-board a special smokescreen-laying boat (Photo: V.G. Yanov, August 1942, from the TsGAKFFD collections, St. Petersburg)

engineer, the commander of the group raising the enemy submarine: "... in spite of a scale 7 near-gale, went out on a dive boat to inspect them and in the course of one night was able to take them off the shallows and deliver them to base."

But at that moment the salvagers were in luck. The Soviet ambassador in Sweden, A.M. Kollontay convinced the Finns to pull out of the war and to conclude a peace treaty with the USSR. Shelling from the Finnish shores ceased immediately, and normal ship-salvage work then proceeded.

The first attempt to raise the boat turned out to be unsuccessful: there were not enough pontoons to break the U-boat off the bottom. Two more had to be added, and the boat floated on four pontoons in all. After this, they additionally fastened it to pontoons sunk to a depth of 29.5 feet, and under the cover of KBF ships and aircraft, pulled it to Kronstadt at a speed of two knots in a space of thirty-five hours, and on September 16, placed it in drydock for inspection and disassembly of the weapons (Fig. 056). But this part of the operation did not involve any diving.

A total of thirty-two days were spent on raising the U-250, but in this time the divers worked underwater for 290 hours. Many of the participants in this operation, unique in its own way, were awarded decorations and medals.

As has already been said, the circumstances at the time the U-250 was raised were quite typical for such work in a zone accessible to the enemy, whether on the open sea as in this case, or in the close

Fig. 056: The German U-250 in drydock, city of Kronstadt.

rear, such as the Volga channel above and below Stalingrad, at Novorossiysk or Sevastopol on the Black Sea, at Kronstadt on the Baltic, or virtually all the fords across rivers. As the front line retreated farther westward, only bombing was left for the Germans, while we could recover.

Underwater operations did not always end as luckily as in the case of the U-250, with hardly any losses. Very often, divers died under enemy fire, and vessels assisting the dives were lost. But the costs were greater for the salvagers, including divers, when providing for emergency salvages during naval landing operations.

There are many examples of this.

Servicing Ships of the Fleet

During the combat actions of ships in both the Navy and the riverine flotillas, they suffered numerous instances of damage, both as a result of enemy shelling and because they ran aground while maneuvering. One of the main tasks for divers was the underwater repair of damaged hulls and screw-steering assemblies while still afloat, without docking

Fig. 057: Diver descending to check whether one of the Northern Fleet submarines is in good repair before a military operation. (Photo: Ye. Khaldey, August 1942, from the RGAKFD collections)

or slipping the ship. Such a repair technique substantially shortened the time for removing the damage and putting the ship back in service, which under wartime conditions was a factor of no little importance.

Both shipboard and port divers solved this problem, both at sea and in the rivers, from the first to the last day of the war. Besides the shallow-water ship repair that has already been mentioned, inspection of the draft portion of ships went on by necessity after ships returned from a deployment, for the purpose of detecting damage not noticed by the ship's crew, as well as a second check-up inspection before going to sea.

Practice showed the particular expediency of having divers look over the hull and out-board submarine systems (screws, submarine anchors, seacocks, and, most importantly, dive planes) before a boat deployed. Such preventative inspections more than once allowed defects to be found and potential accidents to be prevented.

On one submarine, divers inspecting the draft area before a deployment found damage to the screw blades that the crew had not even suspected. On another submarine, divers found an irregularity in the dive planes, which in subsequent sailing could have led to their binding. Divers repeatedly found anchor fastenings destroyed by the cable, while in other cases there was damage to the integrity of the cable itself.

There are dozens of such examples.

Fig. 058: Active military operations in the nearshore zone often led to the hull of a ship touching bottom, damaging the ship's hull and screw-steering assembly. Minor damage was removed by divers from base, without docking or slipping the ship. In the photograph: diver preparing to descend to repair the screw on a torpedo boat. (Photo: G.I. Chertov, 1944, KBF, from the TsGAKFFD collections, St. Petersburg)

It must be noted that shipboard divers occupied a distinct and special place in ensuring the safety of ships of the fleet. When surface ships and submarines encountered the enemy, they invariably received damage from both enemy fire and contact with the bottom during necessary maneuvering in combat. In a developing combat situation, the fate of a ship often depended on ship work done, as a rule, by light divers, since there were usually no resources around capable of coming to the aid of a ship in distress. With shipboard divers battling for its life, holes and punctures from rivets blown out due to shock had to be patched, both inside flooded compartments and out-board of the ship, inspections had to be made and, if possible, the damage the ship had received had to be removed, screws and steering had to be freed of entangling cable, various lines and mechanical conduits inside flooded compartments had to be repaired and reconnected, and so on.

The most widespread type of light-diver operation on all ships was work on clearing the screws of tangled cable and repairing damage to screws and steering gear, and light divers encountered this problem in the very first days of the war.

In July 1941, at the height of combat action, fishing nets got twisted around both screws of one of the gunships. The ship lost power, and this was a great danger, in view of the attacks from unfriendly aircraft. The ship's light divers submerged on a bottom cable to work on freeing the screws. They released the screws using their knives, which took an hour and forty minutes, and the ship, under normal way, not only escaped from the enemy strike but completed its combat mission.

Light divers saved a lot of ships and their crews. During assault landings and the transfer of shorings and various equipment in the Strait of Kerch, on the Volga, and other crossings, many boats (small

Fig. 059: Oxygen-breathing apparatus, found by searchers on the minesweeper ⊠45, sunk by a German U-boat in August 1944 at a depth of seventy feet in the region of Lake Nerva. (Photo from the archives of A.V. Lukoshkov)

subhunters, armored gunboats, etc.) had their screws wound up with various floating objects, as a result of which they were forced to be in a fire zone with no power. In such situations, light divers were saviors in the fullest sense of the word.

Dropping quickly overboard, most often with a breathing apparatus and no suit, light divers freed screws or cleared mechanical seacocks of fish nets, seines, and other floating objects. This saved the boat and provided it the opportunity to complete its assigned combat mission.

Light divering gear is often found on sunken boats (Fig. 059).

Shipboard divers on-board submarines performing a mission played a particularly important role, since in such a situation, the boats were usually engaged in autonomous running and waiting for assistance was not an option. Thus, at the very height of combat actions in 1942, a submarine that was on enemy shores while carrying out a mission was seriously damaged and lost power, steering, and communications.

In view of the absence of communications, there was very little hope of help from the outside. The only possibilities for rescue were: the chance passage of another of our own submarines that happened to be in the vicinity or repair of the damage by our own efforts, and exclusively at night, since working in the daylight was out of the question, in view of the proximity of the enemy shore.

The boat's light divers did all of the repairs, with the support of the machinist mates and torpedomen. In the course of three nights, using a traditional Russian tool (the sledge hammer), as well as a hack

Fig. 060: Practice dive for a shipboard light diver. (Photo: 1943–1944(?), Black Sea Fleet, from the TsVMM collections)

saw and a chisel, they repaired the deformed vertical and horizontal stabilizers, cut off the bent ends of the blades on the screws, and gave the boat the ability to return to base, moving and maneuvering independently, but at low power.

There were more than just a few such cases of repairing screws, steering, and retractable systems on submarines, and fixing submarine damage on a combat deployment was considered an action worthy of a state award.

Because of the small size of light-diver equipment, shipboard divers were utilized for work in flooded compartments with narrow winding passages, where it was impossible for divers to work in ventilated gear.

Thus, in one case, the steering system was heavily damaged due to bombs falling directly onto the stern of a ship, and the steering was jammed in the "hard-over" position. The ship had to go for repair at a safe port, but it couldn't complete its mission, since the ship was drifting sideways with no power, and a tug couldn't come.

Thanks to only the shipboard light divers, who were able to repair the steering system in the steering section, which was flooded with water and cluttered with fragments of metal and wood, the ship regained its normal power and maneuverability.

Compact light-diver equipment allowed for the inspection of a floating dock that had sunk in Nikolayev. In order to get inside the dock through narrow manholes, the divers took off their apparatus and, squeezing the mouthpiece between their lips and holding the apparatus in front of them in their outstretched hands, they passed through into the flooded compartment. And there they continued to work, after fastening their apparatus back on.

A similar problem arose when lifting a floating dock in Novorossiysk. In order to pass through the narrow openings, the divers, who had exhaled beforehand, squeezed the apparatus breathing bag with their hands, expelled the air from it, thus reducing its volume to a minimum, and pushed into a space where they patched holes, opened valves, etc.

And generally, work in narrow waters required of the divers not only personal courage but sometimes extremely non-standard approaches to solving the problem presented. Chief Petty Officer Vladimir Makarovich Mishchenko solved the problem of a passage into the compartment of a dock in his own way:

> While pumping out a dock in a third pontoon, a hose was battered due to the weather and the pump stopped working. It turned out to be impossible to remove the hose for replacement without sending a diver down. It was also impossible to lower divers in ordinary equipment, since a diver could not squeeze through into the neck tube. Chief Petty Officer Mishchenko made a special collar at the forge, and he himself, without diving weights or

> corselet slid through personally into the necktube of the dock's pontoon and freed the damaged hose.

Chief Petty Officer Mishchenko was awarded the medal "For Valor" for this dive.

Sometimes shipboard divers had to carry out unusual tasks. Occasionally during enemy aircraft attacks, fire broke out on a ship, which cut off the exit from the sickbay with injured sailors. An ordinary gas mask could not cope with the heavy smoke, and a shipboard diver went into the sickbay in oxygen apparatus and helped the wounded get out.

There was occasionally work for the light divers on Black-Sea Fleet cruisers that was unusual even for wartime. Due to something that happened, ships were unable to get into a dock for a long time, and their draft would get covered with a thick layer of barnacles, which reduced the ship's rate of travel and its maneuverability.

At that time, every ship was provided with several dozen well-equipped light divers, who were designated to be utilized for cleaning off the ship's draft. The divers went overboard from dinghies. Carefully working on bottom lines, with scrapers or wooden blades so as not to damage the paint, they removed the barnacles and algae that had grown on. We must give its due to the excellent organization of this important procedure; of the many thousands of the divers' underwater descents, there was not a single unlucky case.

It must be pointed out in particular that on ships with a lot of shipboard divers, their principal specialty was something else: bilge machinist mate, deckhand, etc.

But this did not prevent them from going into the water when necessary and carrying out specific diver-related work to save or repair their own ship.

Chapter 5

THE REAR

The front is only the tip of the iceberg during wartime. In order to conduct successful combat actions, every country worked on the needs of the front, and divers in the rear were no exception. Of course, the country without question devoted all its forces to victory, but by the middle of the war, the outcome had already been decided. And even though the road to victory was a long one still, blood was still flowing abundantly and hundreds, thousands, millions of lives were being mourned, more and more resources were being apportioned for the country's future, for its subsequent renaissance.

Rebuilding and Maintaining Seaports and Inland Waterways

The most common type of area where divers worked in the rear and, consequently the objects of diving work, can be divided into two categories: areas where there was no combat action and areas liberated from the Germans.

Ordinary diving work was done in the deep rear. This included laying pipelines, the twin Okha–Sofiysk oil pipeline transit, for instance, across the Nevelskoy Strait, which in 1942 offered an outlet for Sakhalin oil to the mainland, or the underwater pipeline over the bottom of the Caspian Sea and the construction in 1943 of the Astrakhan-Saratov main-trunk petroleum-product pipeline for delivering oil deep in the country to circumvent the water route over the Volga past Stalingrad, which had been cut off by the Germans; the construction of water intakes for defense industries evacuated to the Urals or Siberia; laying down power-supply and communications cables, and so on. With these types of work, the specific nature of the diving had no analogue in peacetime. Really, the divers' labor, like that of the entire country, was regulated in accordance with military law and not that of peacetime, with a more meager supply and provision of engineering materials. But in general and on the whole, safety regulations were observed, which was not always done at the front.

In the rear of our attacking forces, the situation was somewhat different.

A serious problem was the scale of the destruction. In retreating, the Germans had destroyed everything they could. Sunken ships lay in the ports, hindering passage to moorages; the ruins of bridges blown up and ships sunk blocked marine and riverine waterways, making it impossible to cross the rivers, navigate the waterways, or use the ports. This severely complicated the movement of both troops and their supplies, which were all needed for successful combat actions.

The organization of normal work in ports and naval bases, the restoration of the waterways, the reconstruction of railroad and highway bridges and of pipeline and cable crossings at rivers and other water areas were impossible without the wide use of diving operations. In general, normal diving work went on in liberated territories: routine diving, if you can call it that.

In order to restore the destroyed infrastructure on the rivers, beginning in 1942, the Military Reconstruction Administration (VVU) was created along with its subunits, the Military Reconstruction Detachments (VVOs) and the Ship-Salvage Detachments (ASOs). And in June of 1943, based on the decision of the GKO at the Navy Narkomat, a Riverine Ship-Salvage Administration (RASU) was created, whose task included restoration of the river and bridge economy.

At sea, this problem was solved by the divers of the navy's Rescue Service, as the burdens of combat were reduced for them. Thus, after combat actions ended on the Kola Peninsula and in Karelia, the principal efforts of the Northern Fleet diving services were thrown into restoring the infrastructure of those regions. Northern Fleet divers repaired the hydro works of the Tuloma Hydroelectric Power Station and the Niva-2 Hydroelectric Station, they rebuilt the water intakes at Murmansk and Petrozavodsk, as well as all the railroad bridges from Murmansk to Volkhov, and they put the moorages in order in Kola Bay and built new ones in Severomorsk.

As we have already noted, the main problems in the liberated regions were two, from a diving point of view: the presence in the work areas of a huge number of sunken ships and vessels and the destroyed hydraulic works (including bridge spans) and an abundance of objects on the bottom at risk of exploding.

Both marine and riverine sailors began to be involved in serious ship salvage at the end of the war, after the front lines had moved sufficiently far away from where the work was being done, and the navy began to come back to the main naval base on the Black Sea, Sevastopol, and to reclaim ports captured by the enemy, such as the port of Pillau (in the Königsberg–Kaliningrad region). Naturally, the first task was to clear the waterways at the approach to the ports and the waters of the ports themselves, especially at moorages in docking areas, of mines of various types, unexploded ammunition, and flooded, and especially sunken vessels and ships left behind by the enemy.

Inspecting the bottom and draft of ships in the base areas was a preventative measure and, as we would express it today, a kind of counter-terrorist measure. Toward the end of the war, the enemy's "K Command," the unit of German combat swimmers mentioned

Fig. 061: Red Fleet sailor P. Rakovskiy getting a diver, K. Anisimov, ready to inspect the bottom. (Photo: Ye. Khaldey, August 1944, from the RGAKFD collections)

earlier, was already operating on the Baltic. The Germans conducted several successful operations not only against the Allies, but also against our troops as well, blowing up, "... under the very eyes of the Russians, five important bridges, including two at Szczecin and three between the Wolin island and Pomerania," as K. Bekker wrote in his book *German Naval Saboteurs* (Moscow, 1958). And, in principle, we can't forget other sabotage against Soviet ships and port facilities. On the Black Sea itself, when abandoning the port cities, the Germans frequently left explosive "surprises" on the bottom.

Thus, when passing into any waters won back from the Germans, whether a seaport or the water route on a river or lake, the first task for the divers was to clear the bottom of objects likely to explode: unexploded ordnance and especially bottom mines set by the enemy.

A good example is that of finding fougasses in the waters of Feodosia. In the recollections of Oleg Tumanov, a rescue service diver in the Black Sea Fleet, presented in his book *Five Thousand Hours Under Water* (Moscow, Izd. DOSAAF, 1978), while searching for ships and vessels sunk at the port of Feodosia, a cable was found lying on the bottom. One of its ends went to the underwater concrete portion of the port authority basement, the other to a wooden box, in which were found, when it was opened, about 1,763 pounds of TNT. Later, with the support of minemen summoned from Sevastopol, divers

Fig. 062: Raising an unexploded aircraft bomb in the waters of the port of Klaipeda, 1945.

found another three boxes of explosives, attached by cables to a special cut out switch at the port authority. These four boxes were positioned transverse to the port entrance, and the Germans had intended to explode them if we attempted to make an assault landing at the port of Feodosia. Blowing up almost two and a half tons of explosives would have virtually frustrated any attempt to land from that direction.

Feodosia was won back from the Germans in a strike from the land side, and the Germans, departing by sea, simply had not managed to blow up the charges.

The number of shells, bombs, and mines found and disarmed just after the front moved off to the west is simply incalculable, and to this day they are found on the bottom or in nearshore zones. Particularly dangerous were bottom mines that were fitted with special self-destruction devices, and more than one diver died after being blown up by such mines while they were being disarmed.

Furthermore, bottom mines set by the Germans during the war or left during their retreat were very hard to sweep for. So to this day, the favored version of the reason why the battleship *Novorossiysk* blew up in Sevastopol in 1955 is the lack of trawling for bottom mines from the World War II era.

In many waterway areas and in the waters of riverine ports, the Germans sank vessels and barges, blowing them up so as to inflict the

Fig. 063: The destroyer *Svobodnyy* [*Free*], sunk in Korabelnaya Bay, Sevastopol, in June 1942.

maximum possible damage to the hulls of flooded flotation means and thereby making their salvage difficult. A bit under a hundred different vessels were sunk at the river port of Kiev alone, and it was necessary to raise all of them for normal port operations.

The same thing happened at dozens of other river and seaports and stations where the navy was based. All this scrap metal lying on the bottom in waterways and along the moorage walls had to be raised quickly, if only according to a short-term plan, to provide bases for naval ships and facilities for loading and unloading cargo vessels.

A particular problem was clearing the Black Sea Fleet's naval base at Sevastopol. The front line rolled twice through the city and port with fierce fighting, and a multitude of ships, both Soviet and those of the Germans, remained on the bottom and at the moorages of Sevastopol Bay. Departing from Sevastopol, the Germans sank everything that could float, and naturally they sank them in the most inconvenient places.

There was a similar situation in the Baltic ports, like the enemy's naval base at Pillau. During the battles for Pillau (now called Baltiysk), Soviet aircraft operated above the port and adjacent waters of the Baltic Sea, after turning the port itself and its approaches into a graveyard of ships. The density of sunken ships in the waters of Pillau itself and the surrounding waters was extremely high, and in spite of all the efforts made to find and raise them, sunken ships and barges are found to this day, including barges with loaded ammunition, which is really unpleasant.

Fig. 064: Ship raised by KBF divers on side pontoons. (Photo: B.S. Losin, 1943, from the TsGAKFFD collections, St. Petersburg)

Usually when clearing waterways, ship-salvage operations are performed at shallow depths, in waters free of wave swells, in the immediate vicinity of safety on shore. But, on the other hand, when working on the bottom and particularly when carrying out bottom operations, a serious threat always existed of running into unexploded ordnance. The threat was exacerbated by the fact that a shell shot or a bomb dropped that did not explode for some reason, released all its safety mechanisms the instant it was fired or dropped and could literally explode at the slightest vibration or shift. Such unexploded ordnance did not always blow up, but it sometimes happened, and it was impossible to predict how the ammunition would react when recovered.

We stated before that there were two theaters for diving operations, at sea and in the inland reservoirs. Sometimes operations on the rivers proceeded under much more difficult conditions than at sea. The current, low visibility or its complete absence, and the high amount of debris on the bottom made dives considerably harder, and the volume of work that had to be accomplished was colossal.

Routes of communication during World War II were of special significance. The attacking portion of the Red Army moved along them; military equipment, ammunition, and products were transported to the front, communications were established between the front and the rear, and the command authorities for German forces, understanding this, took every possible opportunity to destroy them when retreating.

Fig. 065: Temporary pontoon bridge across the Danube in the region of Budapest. Building such a bridge restored automobile traffic but blocked the water route, and motor vehicle traffic had to be stopped and the bridge raised for ships to pass through. (Photo: February 1945, from the RGAKFD collections)

In addition, water routes for communication also had a purely military significance. Moving along the rivers, the riverine military flotillas supported the operational forces with fire from shipboard artillery and with assault landings, and the enemy tried in every possible way to block the water routes by mining waterways and swamping vessels in the shallows.

Bridges over the entire extent of the front line were blown up twice: first by our troops when retreating at the beginning of the war, and then by the Germans during their retreat in the second half of the war. Blowing up bridges immediately solved two problems at once: it destroyed the land routes (highway and railroad) and the water routes of communication.

Divers in the Riverine Ship-Salvage Administration, created in 1943, cleared the inland waterways of sunken ships, destroyed bridge spans, and a huge number of mines and unexploded ordnance.

The bridges were rebuilt in three stages. The first-stage was to put the highways and railroads back in working order in the shortest time possible in order to provide the Red Army with everything it needed. Here, the waterways remained blocked, as a rule. This work was done under near-front conditions, under artillery fire and enemy bombardment, and often without considering the losses.

In the second stage, right after the front moved farther west, bridges were reconstructed on pilings, although on a temporary plan,

Fig. 066: Separating a girder from a bridge across the Western Dvina (Daugava) River in Riga, which had collapsed as a result of an explosion.

but still on a full-scale basis, ensuring movement not only by land but to a certain extent by water transport. At the same time, with the goal of unblocking the waterways, the collapsed spans and supports of an old bridge blown up in the course of combat action were dismantled, and this was the most complicated and hazardous operation, from the point of view of practical diving.

Dive groups in riverine bridge-salvage detachments executed underwater operations under exceptionally difficult conditions. Dives were made in currents of up to 6.5 ft./sec or more, the water was so murky that visibility was practically nil, and work had to be done by feel. The Germans additionally mined many bridges after blowing them up, and divers had to clear them of mines first. Of course, the girders of the collapsed bridges themselves were a complex accumulation of metal, whose sharp edges could cut through air hoses and signal lines in an instant and trigger entrapment or even death for a diver.

F.I. Krylov, leader of the GVRU, describes work on rebuilding one of the bridges:

> The complexity of conducting diving operations under such conditions can be illustrated by the following example. To provide for ship passage on the River Sozh at Gomel', it was necessary to clear a passageway where a metal highway bridge had collapsed. The iron girders had been torn apart and

tossed into the water; the bridge buttresses were also ripped apart. A complex accumulation of girder metal and reinforced concrete had formed at the bottom of the river. Individual elements, the stanchions and braces, projected out above the water and hindered the movement of vessels.

Some 82–98 feet from the bridge centerline, which had been torn down by the road units of the 1st Belorussian Front, a temporary, high-water wooden bridge was erected on a base of pilings. A GVRU unit was ordered to dismember the collapsed structure by means of explosions and to sink it at the bottom of the river, thereby ensuring the safety of the vessels passing through.

In view of the proximity of the new bridge, the weight of the charge was limited to a dozen kilograms. It was proposed to first blow up the stanchions and braces projecting out of the water.

The work was done by a single dive station. After the first explosion, the section commander, diver P.Ya. Narozhnyy went down to inspect the results of the explosion. One stanchion continued to stand up vertically, and Comrade Narozhnyy got the impression that the stanchion, with a double-T cross-section, was not going to break apart with explosives. But he just touched the stanchion and it was enough for it to change position and press him against the lower boom of the girder.

Fortunately, his air hoses were not broken. Comrade Narozhnyy reported what had happened without delay, phoning to the group commander. The closest dive station was a distance of thirty-one miles from the work site, and its assistance might be delayed. As he was in a touch-and-go position, the diver lost no time: he used the line they had given him for signaling, and with great effort strapped up the stanchion, which was pinning his legs down. They lifted the stanchion, after which the diver surfaced. After being treated in hospital for several days, Comrade Narozhnyy continued diving.

This case taught the detachment's personnel component a lot. It is true, that in a subsequent operation, work proceeded with one dive station present, since the full strength of groups with dive stations in 1945, like in 1944, did not exceed 55%. But the situation required the timely conduct of underwater operations on objects whose number considerably exceeded the number of bridge-salvage groups.

Fig. 067: Diving operations restoring a bridge across the Dnepr River. (Photo: T. Sedykh, May 1945, from the RGAKFD collections)

The third stage of restoration was the capital reconstruction of bridges, usually carried out just in the far rear of the attacking/assault forces.

Oftentimes, it was not a simple matter to unblock a waterway, and other variants had to be sought for the passage of military ships along the river channels. So when battles raged along the rivers, flotilla ships had to pass by the Western Bug and go from there to the mouth of the Narew River, where the flotilla was to be included in combat actions, fifty-eight miles away, but on this route, blown-up bridges blocked the rivers, and the depth at the sandbars often did not reach eleven inches. Besides, the draft of an armored gunboat, even when unloaded, is about half a meter.

All this demanded that special measures be taken. They loaded light diver-sappers with charges and they blew up the underwater obstacles. A bridge-salvage detachment extracted the bridge girders dismembered by the explosions out of the water and pulled down the rock fragments and flushed out the sand bars using a hydraulic excavator. All this provided a corridor for ship passage.

It sometimes happened that the situation required laying out a new water route, such as during the Leningrad blockade. In order for ships going to sea on the southern waterway past Kotlin island (where Kronstadt is located) to withdraw from under enemy artillery fire, it was decided to clear the ship passage of old hydraulic-engineering equipment from as long ago as the time of Peter the Great. This path was north of the island, outside the zones that enemy artillery could reach. A very short period of time was set for this work by decree of the Baltic Fleet Military Council.

The work was so important for organizing the defense of Leningrad that those who took part in it received State awards. On the award citation for a dive-station petty officer who accomplished this work, the following was stated:

> Petty Officer Comrade P.V. Sirotkin, performing his duty as leader of the dive group, personally worked under water in wintertime conditions. He provided training for the explosion of crib obstacles, and after pulling more than 328 cubic feet of stone out of the crib sections, he laid up to twenty-five tons of explosives on the crib grates, at risk to his life, placing primers to ensure the explosions would occur simultaneously.
>
> As dive group-leader, he used the icy conditions to advantage, he organized the work of the personnel complement subordinate to him and completed the mission to blow up a portion of the crib obstacles, built in the years of 1851–1861, fifteen days ahead of the deadline set by the plan. Under his leadership, the divers worked up to fourteen hours a day underwater.

Working at night in murky water and zero visibility, the diver manually pulled the fill out of fourteen crib grates 5.9 x 5.9 feet in cross-section and at a depth of up to eighteen feet and laid down thirty-seven tons of explosives on them. With the simultaneous explosion of all the charges, a passage was formed 328 feet wide and nineteen feet deep, thanks to which small

Fig. 068: Dive station for the Main Riverine Administration, at a reconstructed wharf wall on the Moscow Canal. (Photo: end of the 1940s, from the archives of V.P. Kozlov, diving specialist)

military craft could exit to the sea, secretly and unhindered by the enemy.

But let us turn now to the territories, or more accurately the waters, won back from the enemy. There, as we have already said, the minimum necessary ship-passages were cleared first. The free passage space thus gained was less than that before the war in both breadth and depth, but even so it allowed the through-passage of ships on the principal water routes in the Don–Kuban, Dnepr, and Dnepr–Dvina basins.

Thus, as the end of the war approached, the volume of diving work that needed to be done grew precipitously, and it was not surprising that divers came to be in tragically short supply, especially considering the dearth of men caused by losses at the front. Therefore, to provide for dive work, women had to be widely enlisted as pumpers on the manual dive pumps and as phone operators, leaving the men for just on-the-spot underwater work. But the women's labor, of course, did not solve the problems with the cadres, and all those elements interested in diving operations began to take the most resolute steps to train qualified divers, and the closer the end of the war came, the more active they were.

Fig. 069: Student practice descents at the diving range on Lake Baykal.

Diver Training

There are no statistics today on losses among the divers, but it is known that they were high. The conditions of military actions often necessitated conducting diving operations under enemy attacks, and the pure hazards of diving were added to all the associated danger. Many divers died at their dive sites, under water, from the effects of a shock wave from underwater explosions, they exhausted the air in their diving dress on the bottom after their dive boats succumbed, they suffered decompression sickness after the dive boat, running from enemy attack, virtually "yanked" them to the surface in the process, without the necessary decompression.

In the initial period of the war, the needs of the cadres, caused both by the expanding of the field of activity for the dive groups and by losses among the divers, were compensated for with the reserve trained before the war, both officers and enlisted, and later at the rear, at diving schools and in Navy courses, the Corps of Engineers, and the OSVOD Union, as well as on-the-job training in the fleets and in the army in the field.

The main "forge for the cadres" remained the navy's Emergency-Rescue Training Detachment, the former Balaklava Naval Diving Technical School of EPRON.

In the very beginning of the war, the detachment remained in Balaklava, although the students in the detachment went to war in the

Fig. 070: Capt. 2nd Rank M.P. Avgustinovich, commander of a Northern Fleet submarine, conducting diving classes in the pool. (Photo: 1943, from the RGAKFD collections)

first days in an infantry unit, as foot soldiers. And only the extreme need for divers for clearing Sevastopol Bay of the non-contact bottom mines being dropped by the Germans from aircraft were command authorities forced to turn to the EPRON divers to use them in their true specialty.

Toward the end of 1941, the military situation in Balaklava forced the Navy Narkom to decide to transfer the training detachment to Astrakhan. But it turned out to be impossible to train specialists there in the normal way.

In 1942, N.P. Chiker, the representative of the navy's Emergency Rescue Service organized the base transfer of the diving school to Lake Baykal. Very quickly, the school cadets and instructors built barracks, classrooms, and workshops at the new site and fitted out a training area for practical exercises.

The onset of the Siberian winter was associated with great hardship, with cold down to minus 86°F or lower. In the open air, valves froze and failed, diving suits froze through and ripped, ice plugs formed in the hose connections and then in the hoses. In order to create more or less normal conditions for diving, little temporary heated huts had to be set above the ice holes and stoves in them had to be fired up when diving.

In parallel with the training process, the specialists at the diving school frequently had to take part in emergency-rescue and ship-salvage operations in Lake Baykal, exploding rock bars on the Angara, and carrying out other underwater engineering operations.

In 1944, after the liberation of the Crimea, by order of the Soviet Navy Narkom, the diving school was turned back over to the Black Sea Fleet. Once again, the training base, which had been destroyed, was rebuilt through the efforts of the school's personnel complement, and a training range was built for the divers.

But the student strength of the detachment was not enough to cover the needs of the fleet for divers, and in 1943–1944, short diving courses were organized in units of the navy ERS and on navy ships.

The young divers, the graduates of these courses, handled simple work, but they had little experience, and they had to institute subsequent practical training for them under operating conditions. For this, a diving probation period was introduced in the fleets, during which for three to four months, a diver-probationer picked up stable operational habits, and the qualification of "diver" was given for the time he had already served. The very first experiment in diving probation proved its value so well that it was subsequently introduced for all the diving elements being trained, including for the normal training going on at the navy ASUO.

A great deal of attention was paid to training contingency divers, usually light divers, for the elements and ships of the fleets. As a rule, training this category of diver, as well as diver training for combat unit BCh-5 officers, top physician elements, and ship doctors was accomplished at annual assemblies and at various courses, as well as directly in the fleets. In 1945, in the first years after the war, the ASUO VMS organized the training of 2nd class divers, who, having mastered new methods for diving operations and new models of diving equipment, went out to the fleets and flotillas as diving petty officers.

Also in 1945, the first post-war courses for specialist divers were organized. Upon finishing their expert practicum, the diver chief and master chief petty officers received officer rank. Thus, the navy emergency rescue service at least supplied itself and the other navy services with qualified divers.

Diver training was accomplished both in the rear and in the fleets. In the fleets, they trained not only "ventilated" divers, who learned all types of underwater engineering operations including hydraulic engineering, but also light divers, ship divers whose role in the battle of surviving damage received during the combat deployments of surface ships and submarines was exceptionally great.

Fleet command authorities considered this work important and worthy of mention in award citations. Here are a few excerpts from them.

Petty Officer Mikhail Makarovich Lyashenko, commander of a dive section, was awarded the Nakhimov Medal: "In the days of the Patriotic War as an instructor of light diving, he taught sixty-five light divers for Baltic Fleet ships and thereby contributed to increasing their survivability."

Master Chief Petty Officer Leonid Gur'yanovich Molchanov, Diving Petty Officer, KBF, was awarded the Order of the Patriotic War 2nd Degree: "During the years of the Patriotic War, Comrade Molchanov, who was an experienced diving specialist, trained dozens of divers, who are currently successfully handling command tasks."

Petty Officer Sergey Petrovich Miroshnichenko, Acting Petty Officer of Dive Command, MVB-3, Northern Fleet ASO: "He personally trained more than 100 light divers for Northern Fleet ships, having effectively introduced light diving to the fleet."

Lt. Pavel Panteleyevich Konstantinov, diving specialist, Northern Fleet Emergency Rescue Section: "Under his personal leadership, more than 100 light divers and over thirty divers (electrical-arc welders and cutters) were trained in the North."

And even so, there were not enough divers either at the front or in the rear and, it seems there was a very acute need for divers in the army. This was certainly associated with the fact that in the land-based forces, with the constant lack of personnel, especially in the initial period of the war, the troop commands were extremely strongly tempted to throw everyone into battle who could hold a rifle, and it was unimportant whether you were a diver or not. Also possibly associated with this was the lack of success for those repeated attempts to create specialized diver sabotage-recon units. Only extreme need was able to force commanders to utilize divers for their true purpose.

Today, there are no reliable data on the system for training enlisted divers for the Red Army. The OSVOD Union probably played a substantial role in this, as it had traditionally trained pre-conscription divers for the army and navy and continued to so during the war.

The commands of army diving units trained the Corps of Engineers themselves at their own training facilities. It is known that in 1942 the training of officer divers was organized for pontoon units at the Leningrad Military Engineering School, which was evacuated to Kostroma. We recall, by the way, that the first to address this problem of training divers was the Leningrad Military Engineering School as early as the beginning of the 1930s, as we mentioned earlier.

In the graduating class of August–November 1942, in contrast to the prewar training course, principal attention was paid, not to

Fig. 071: Female instructor from the OSVOD Union getting N. Tagil, a light-diver cadet in pre-conscription training, ready for a dive. (Photo: 1943, from the RGAKFD collections)

aspects of sabotage and reconnaissance but to the diving engineer securing fords: raising sunken pontoons, tanks, and other military equipment; breaking apart sunken metal structures such as bridges destroyed in the water, using underwater explosions; building up temporary bridge pilings, clearing the bottom at crossings, constructing moorages, etc.

In all, 128 men were selected for training; they went through theoretical training and practical exercises. Theory included the physiology of diving and a general understanding of diving medicine, the study of diving gear and equipment, and the technology of performing underwater engineering work. Practical exercises were done at the training ground in one of the lakes near the city. The study program lasted 224 hours, and included fifteen hours of diving proper and work underwater for each cadet.

The cadets' training was inscribed in the personal records of courses completed: "They are trained for commanding platoons in engineering units and have practical experience in carrying out engineering work. In addition, they can be utilized as heads of dive stations in engineering units."

It is not known whether this training for diving officers was systematic or whether it was a unique, one-time measure, but there were not enough divers in the army's engineering units, tragically. We have already noted, by way of example, the fact of the absence of divers provided to set up crossings. The head of the Corps of Engineers, 7th Guard Army, in December 1943, in his report to Headquarters, Corps of Engineers for the 2nd Ukrainian Front regarding the engineering provided for forcing the Dnepr river, wrote about how poorly the pontoon units were provided with diving resources: "One diving dress in poor repair for two battalions." The role and importance of dive stations in reconstructing the pontoon depot was high, in the opinion of the head of the Corps of Engineers, 7th Guard Army.

But the training of divers was not limited to the efforts of the navy and the Corps of Engineers. The OSVOD Union, the prewar analogue of DOSAAF in the second half of the twentieth century, played a large role in training divers, mainly light divers.

The main task of OSVOD elements in the years of 1942–1943 was not so much in organizing the rescue of people suffering calamities in the water, saving valuable equipment and military cargo that had sunk, or clearing reservoirs, but principally in training cadres for the army and navy.

A pre-conscript recalled the beginning of the war: "It was like that with us too, a group of pre-conscripts who had just finished tenth grade. They didn't take us into the army early, but sent us to OSVOD to study in light diving courses, since, according to our service registration card, we were to do our military service in the fleet. Of course, to be a sailor is honorable, and who of us didn't dream of that. But for me, somehow it was not my thing: people were fighting for the Motherland, we were quietly diving into Klyazma Reservoir, and when they would call us up, no one knew."

For example, the Moscow OSVODers alone trained hundreds of divers for the army and navy, and there were dozens of such organizations throughout the entire territory of the Soviet Union. So the OSVOD contribution to training divers was extremely substantial.

However, in spite of all the efforts described above, there were still not enough divers. Furthermore, there were not enough "ace" divers and diving specialists who had stuck around for more than a year of training. Indeed, there were very few ace divers and engineering technicians in underwater engineering like E.Ye. Leybovich, P.N. Nikol'skiy, N.V. Sokolov, and a number of others; they had "trotted" them off to the most important objectives all over the whole Soviet Union.

Production of Gear and Equipment

No less strained than with the cadres was the situation that developed in providing the diving services with technical materiel. Significant losses in diving equipment in the first years of the war could not be compensated for. The country's industry was working on the needs of the front, and there were no resources left for diving. N.P. Chiker writes that: "... the output of emergency-rescue equipment was accomplished only by special government decree and in limited quantities. In 1942, the ERS succeeded in placing orders with eleven factories."

This was not sufficient, and non-specialized workshops in the navy's rescue service had to be appealed to for the production of equipment.

In 1942 too, the ERS administration organized the manufacture of new rescue and ship-salvage equipment at its own factory in Moscow.

By order of the State Defense Committee, a Palace of the Soviets construction factory at Luzhniki was handed over for this purpose to the management of the navy ERS. The factory produced forty- and eighty-ton ship-salvage pontoons, motor-driven suction and other pumps, diver's helmets, and various emergency-rescue equipment.

In 1943, Moscow Plant No.3 was handed over subordinate to the ERS, and it was also repurposed to produce emergency-rescue equipment. Its production consisted of bilge ejectors, Cox hole-punch pistol-grip guns, motor-driven compressors, air-distribution panels, and so on. They also expanded production volume at industrial enterprises that were being attracted to this work. By the end of 1943, twenty plants were already filling ERS orders; their product inventory included ninety-one items, and their production volume was six times the 1942 level. Even so, the needs of the ERS units were not adequately provided for, and apparently the supply of Lend-Lease equipment had a measurable role in equipping our diving units.

Lend-Lease

Besides equipment manufactured in domestic factories, the army and navy diving services were also equipped with imported underwater engineering resources. In 1943, a group of specialists was sent to the United States to purchase motor-driven suction pumps, electrical suction pumps, compressors, welding units, and other equipment, and soon the purchases of equipment began to arrive through Baku, Arkhangelsk, and Murmansk to the ERS units.

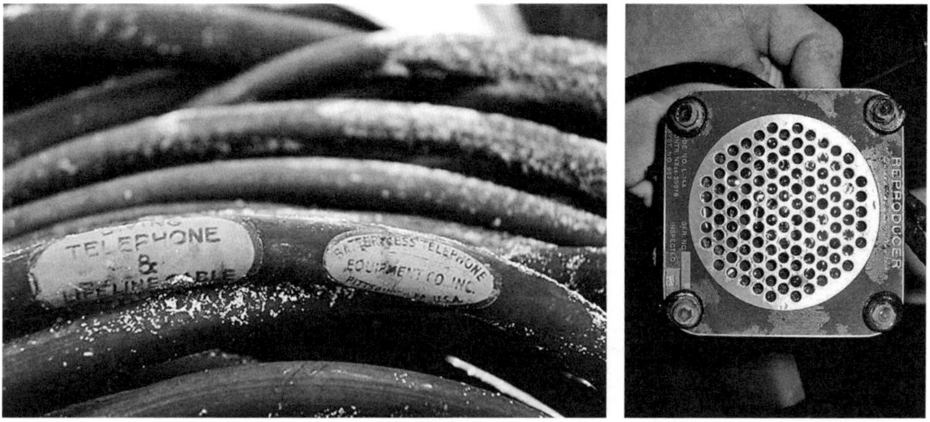

Fig. 072: American signal cable and loudspeaker for a dive telephone post found by searchers on one of the sunken pontoon barges in the Leningrad region.

Lend-Lease played a substantial role in the course of the war. There is quite a lot of information on the volume of Lend-Lease deliveries of equipment and weapons, but it has still not been possible to find any sort of specific data on diving equipment. Nevertheless, it is known that American diving equipment and gear arrived in the Soviet Union. So far, searchers have found on sunken vessels from the wartime, and roaming about in the hands of diving history enthusiasts: American helmets, diving knives, and other pieces of foreign diving gear from the war days. Chiker, who has already been mentioned several times, writes in his book *The Special-Operations Service* (Moscow, 1975) that: "... in the war years ... a large amount of diving equipment ... was received from the US. From the middle of 1944 on, imported equipment began to arrive in ample quantity." Apparently the diving equipment came to us not only by direct delivery, but also on ships and vessels being purchased for shipboard dive stations, or in kits with American engineering equipment that arrived for the army (Fig. 072).

One way or another, American diving gear and equipment came to us, but our cooperation with the Americans on diving was not limited to this.

In the war years, we also received literature and materials from the US on their experience with underwater operations, the education of the diving component in diving, including deep-water dives, diving equipment, medical supplies, etc. These books were translated here and issued.

Fig. 073: Soviet naval officers in class at an American diving school.

Specialized Knowledge

As we have already said, toward the middle of the war, in 1943–1944, its outcome had already become clear, and the opportunity came to the commands of the armed forces to think about the post-war build-up of trusted authorities, including those of the diving services.

On December 1, 1944, the head of the Navy General Staff published a circular on "Organizational-Staff Changes in the Navy's Emergency Rescue Service," in which, among other measures, "the formation of a scientific-research institute for the Emergency Rescue Service" was ordered, to be subordinate to the head of the navy ERS.

This was in principle an important step, and the scientific-research organization created just seventy years ago, and to this day, in spite of all the twists and turns of the last decades, it is playing an enormous role in the development of diving and emergency rescue in this country.

Specialized sections entered into the structure created in 1944, which is now called the Scientific-Research Institute of Rescue and Underwater Technology: emergency rescue, ship salvage, diving, underwater electrical engineering and instruments, and diving medicine. Several vessels were also attached to the institute for practical development tests under water of new technologies and equipment created by the institute.

In these years too (1943–1944), specialty literature began to be published on diving, and toward 1945, toward the end of the war, twenty-seven books, manuals, regulations, and instructions were issued, such as: *Oxy-Fuel Cutting of Steel Under Water* by D.L. Glizmanenko, *Underwater Explosive Work by* P.G. Radevich, *Underwater Engineering* by S.Ya. Mal'tsev, *Manual on Emergency Rescue, Ship Salvage, and Diving* by a group of authors, in three volumes, *Regulations for the Diving Service* in four parts, *Instructions for Aligning a Rubble Base and Planning Slopes,* and others. A series of books came out in 1946.

From 1943 on, the publication of information bulletins was resumed, of *Navy ERS Papers,* averaging three issues a year. Printed in the papers were both practical articles on new methods of executing underwater operations, domestic and imported equipment (such as "Oxy-Hydrogen Cutting," "Technology of Underwater Electric-Arc Welding," and "Electric-Arc Welding Underwater," articles on ship salvage, repair of ships and vessels afloat, bottom operations, and others), and articles on perspectives for the development of diving, such as N.A. Klimenko's article "Diving: State-of-the-Art and Perspectives."

Articles in the papers on practical operations on sunken objects, which bore, according to the unwritten rules of the war years, the nature of victory reports, nevertheless shed light in detail on problems that arose in performing ship repairs, ship salvage, and underwater engineering, and offered recommendations for avoiding such situations. Special attention was paid to issues of electric-arc welding and cutting underwater, which was double the current number, since the volume of work on disassembly of vessels and metal hydraulic-engineering structures blown up and sunk by the enemy during retreat was simply enormous.

Such an approach to supplying the material made the papers very useful to practitioners in the fleets and flotillas. In the second half of the war, work on the creation of new equipment was started up again, which had been interrupted by the war. Modifications to the ISA oxygen breathing apparatus were worked out and set into production, which received the designation of ISA-M (or ISA-M43) with improved use characteristics, as well as underwater lamps for general and local illumination, several types of dive telephone posts, and many others. The work on restoration was actively performed on a domestic-element basis for equipment being received by Lend-

Fig. 074: Publication of scientific and technical literature on diving was already being started up again by the middle of the war.

Lease. So the Cox hole-punch pistol-grip guns were mastered in production, as well as the MVTS-3v diving loudspeaker telephone posts, and many other things.

Today, looking back on those times and having before us the evolution of diving in this country in the post-war years up to the end of the twentieth century, it may confidently be said that the correct and visionary organizational, scientific, and technical policy chosen in the second half of the war provided domestic diving in the 1950s to 1970s with stable development and an advanced position in the world with respect to a number of issues.

Chapter 6

EQUIPMENT AND WEAPONS

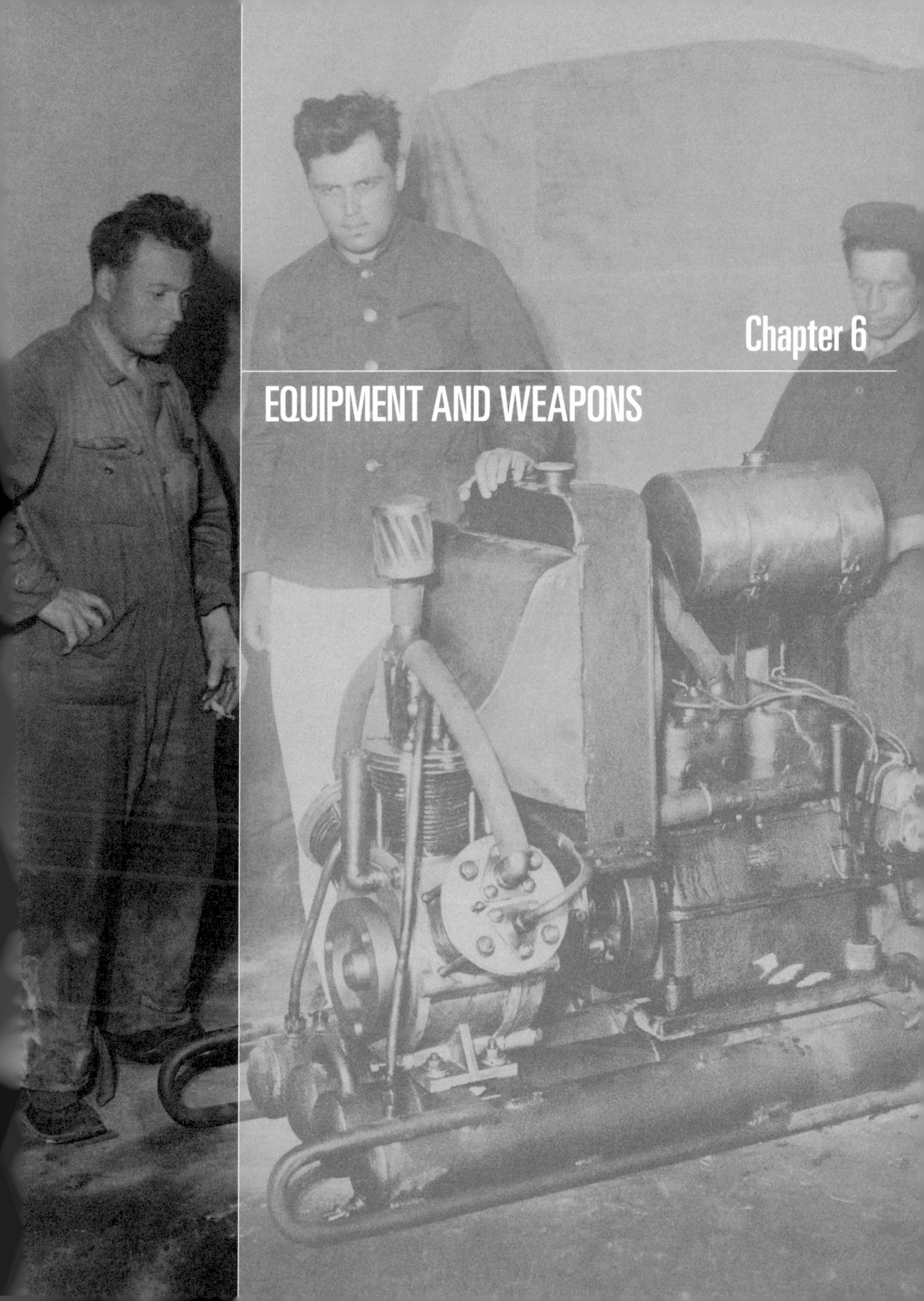

The diving elements entered the war comparatively well outfitted. All the basic types of diving gear and equipment in the country were in series production; in many ways, it was of better quality than similar ones abroad.

There is quite a lot of information on precisely what gear the divers used during the war; in general, it is entirely authentic, although it is hard to say how exhaustive it is. Historians of domestic diving, when researching what divers worked on during the war, rely today on various sources of information that fall into several groups.

First there is the literature of manuals and handbooks. The nomenclature for gear used in the war period was defined by the *Regulations for the Diving Service*, 1944 edition (in Part II, *Dives in Close-Circuit Underwater Apparatus*, and in Part IV, *Dives in Lightweight Diving Suit (OVS), Harbor Mask, and Rigid Diving Dress*). Diving gear used during dives is also described in volume 2 of the *Manual on Emergency Rescue and Diving*, published in 1945, and in the corresponding technical descriptions and handbooks for using individual types of diving gear and equipment.

The recollections of war veterans are a second source of information. As a rule, memoirs are accurate enough, although it happens that memory sometimes betrays the veterans. For instance, in the dives of the 1943–1944 years, they sometimes state that the ISA-M-48 oxygen apparatus was used, although that appeared right after the war, whereas the ISA-M apparatus was used in those years (or, as it was sometimes called, the ISA-M-43).

Photographs of divers are a third source of information, taken during training for a dive or during the dive, in which the equipment used can be identified.

And finally, serving as an extremely valuable source of information are the individual items of diving gear preserved in museum collections or found by searchers on board sunken ships and submarines.

Analysis of all this information in its entirety gives us an opportunity to imagine rather clearly what divers worked in World War II.

Diving Gear

Ventilation Equipment

The predominant volume of diving work during wartime was accomplished in ventilated diving gear. Unfortunately, in the documentary manuals and handbooks already cited, only a certain generalized description is given for the gear developed by EPRON engineers in the prewar years, although it is known that divers also

Fig. 075: Helmet that came out at the beginning of the twentieth century. (Detail, photo: Ye. Khaldey, August 1942, from the RGAKFD collections)

used the equipment of other manufacturers, including that produced just before the Revolution.

It would seem possible to determine the type of gear used from the photographs from that time. But first of all, very few of them are preserved, and secondly, only the types of helmet used can be more or less unimpeachably determined on that basis. It is impossible to identify the type, manufacturer, and "age" of a manual dive pump from photographs; all the pumps are externally too similar to one another. And dive suits generally are in essence made of very expendable material, especially for active work, and no sort of identification can be made based on photographs .

The helmets of ventilated diving gear are simple in construction and are made of corrosion-resistant copper (helmet body and corselets)

Fig. 076: Sh-3 helmet developed by EPRON in the middle of the 1930s. (Photo: 1943, practice dive by a cadet in the ASUO, Soviet Navy)

and brasses (parts of fastenings, valve parts, air and cable feeds). With good care, helmets do not wear out, and they can be used, and indeed are, used for decades.

The very old helmets, which are depicted in photographs from the war years, were apparently produced back in the beginning of the 1900s. This can be determined from the ports for the acoustic air hose (Fig. 075), which was installed on helmets manufactured by the Izhorskiye Admiralty Plants and the Ye.V. and V.V. Kolbas'yevyy Brothers Kronstadt Experimental Mechanical and Diving Workshop at the end of the 1890s to the beginning of the 1900s. After the appearance of dive telephones, the ports for the acoustic hoses were repurposed as cable inlets, but the port itself, which remained in place, serves as good identification.

The next domestic helmet for ventilated equipment was developed by EPRON in the mid 1930s. These helmets were produced in three- and twelve-bolt variants (Fig. 076).

Besides the domestic variant, divers in the war period also used imported gear delivered before the war: six- and twelve-bolt issue from the English firm of Siebe Gorman & Co. and three-bolt helmets manufactured by the Ravensburg plant in the city of Kiel, Germany, on a French Denayrouze license.

Aside from those cited, two more sources existed for diving gear: these were the Lend-Lease supplies from the Allies and German trophies.

Meanwhile, no data have been found on the types and quantities of gear supplied in Lend-Lease delivery catalogues. Nevertheless, it is know that the gear arrived in Russia and it evidently went into the content of shipboard dive stations or into the property of pontoon units of the RKKA engineers. One way or another, throughout all of Russia, the American twelve-bolt MkV Mod I helmet made by the Desco Company came and stills come today (but only to museums and private collections) (Fig. 077).

Trophy equipment (as a rule, the three-bolt gear from Draeger) began to appear in the second half of the war as German forces retreated, but again there unfortunately are no data on quantities.

Fig. 077: American Mk V, Mod 1 helmet. Helmets like this came into Russia in supplies from the Allies.

Light Diving Gear

Toward the beginning of the war, several types of closed circuit, oxygen-breathing apparatus and two types of drysuit were adopted into the equipment of diving elements in the Red Army and the navy.

During the war, the light divers of the army and navy used IPA-2, IPA-3, VIA-2, and ISA types of oxygen-breathing apparatus (in 1943, the ISA-M or, as it is sometimes called, the ISA-M-43 apparatus was delivered). Several models of breathing apparatus from the wartime have come down to our day. Some were and are found in the repositories of museums; some were found by searchers in ships and submarines lost during the war (Fig. 078).

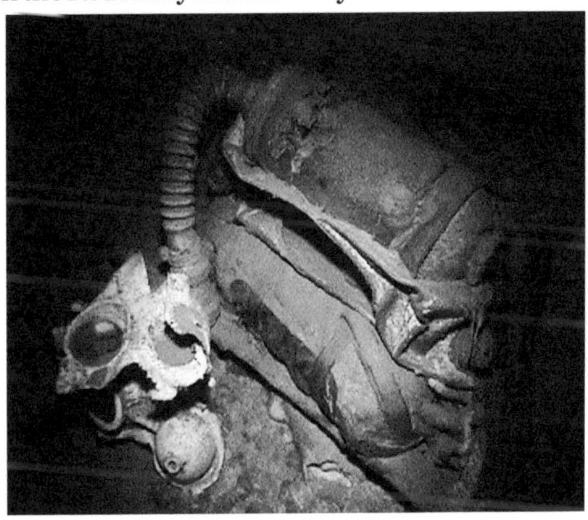

Fig. 078: Oxygen-breathing apparatus found by searchers on board the sunken submarine Shch212. (Photo: A. Kurakin)

Zhiv'yem today preserves the IPA-2, IPA-3, and ISA-M apparatus, as well as the technical specifications and instructions for using the IPA-1, IPA-2, IPA-3, ISA-M, and VIA-2 apparatus.

The principal distinction between the various oxygen-breathing apparatus used during the war was in the arrangement for the oxygen-supply mechanism and the exhaust safety valves on the breathing bags. Without going into detail, we only point out that all this oxygen breathing apparatus (see Table) differed little from one another in their technical and use characteristics or even in their external appearance. Only the IPA-2 apparatus, with its rigid aluminum, rather than a soft rubber-fabric, breastplate, as was adopted later, and the ISA-M (Fig. 079) apparatus are well differentiated, based on the characteristic lobed exhaust valve on the breathing bag.

Parameter	IPA-2	IPA-3	VIA-2	ISA-M (ISA-M-43)
Year produced	before 1936		before 1938	
Oxygen supply regulator	dosage head marked off for O_2 consumption	before dive on test stand	dosage head marked off for O_2 consumption	before dive on test stand
Bypass	yes	yes	yes	yes
Minimum pressure indicator	yes	yes	no	yes
Tank capacity, liters	0.7/1.3	0.7/1.3	0.7/1.3	1.3
Tank pressure, atm.	150	150	150	150
Volume (capacity) of calc. chemical-absorbent cartridge, kg	1.5		1.5–1.8	
Bag volume, liters	10	6.3	8	8
Bag safety valve	combo	combo	combo	automatic
Bag exhaust valve				manual
Breastplate	rigid	soft	soft	soft
Helmet type	goggles with pressure compensator	ShV-2	ShV	ShV-3

Comparative Characteristics of Oxygen-Breathing Apparatus from the End of the 1930s to the beginning of the 1940s

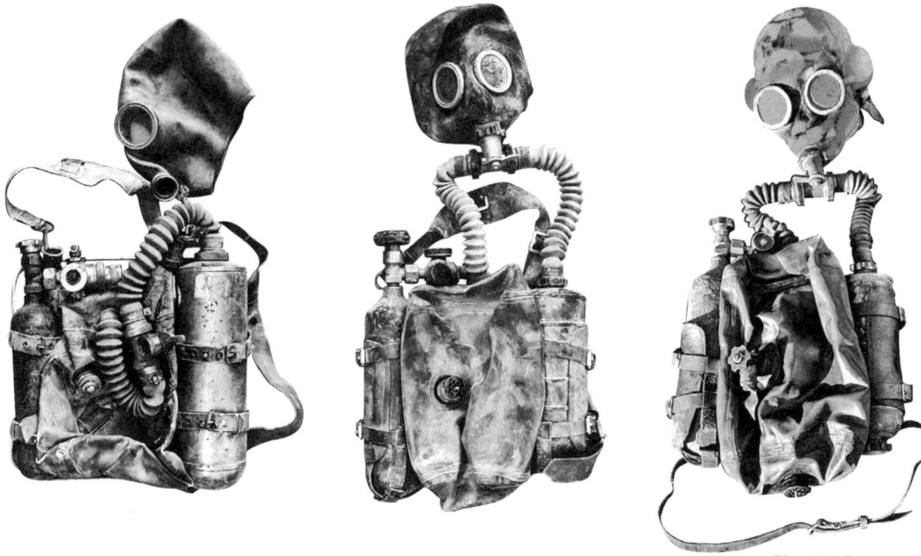

Fig. 079: Oxygen-breathing apparatus used by light divers in the Soviet Navy and Red Army during World War II. On the left, the IPA-2; in the center, the IPA3 (both from the VIMAIViVS collections); and on the right, the IPA-M (found by searchers on a boat sunk in the Gulf of Finland during the war).

Two models of drysuit were used in light-diving equipment during the war, which were created at the end of the 1930s: types E and TU-1. Both drysuits consisted of a blouse with trousers, constructed as one piece. The trousers ended with boots for walking on the bottom, while the blouse was sealed with close-fitting wrists or with sleeves or rubber gauntlets built in. A chest hose-appendix was worn across both drysuits, which was then laced up with a special leakproof rubber cord.

The difference between the type E and type TU-1 drysuits (Fig. 080) was in the construction of the helmet and the appendix.

The E drysuit did not actually have a helmet. It was fitted with a soft rubber helmet-liner with an open face part, which fitted the diver's head tightly. When diving, the diver used a breathing apparatus with a box mouthpiece and a series ShV rubber mask-helmet attached to it, which was worn over or under the drysuit helmet-liner. The appendix was covered with a protective dickey after lacing it up.

The soft helmet liner, which hermetically compressed the diver's head and the mask-helmet worn over it, led to the pressure of residual air between the eardrum and the drysuit helmet liner being lower than the pressure of the surrounding water and consequently lower than the pressure of the air being breathed, which was supplied to the inner ear of the diver. This often led to barotrauma of the ear.

In addition, the compression of the diver's head by two layers of rubber, the helmet liner, and the mask-helmet, led to severe discomfort and as a result, to the diver rapidly becoming fatigued. Divers in the RON were particularly aware of this drawback, since they had to spend many hours in a drysuit, if not all day.

Fig. 080: A Type E drysuit (on the left) and a TU-1 suit (on the right). On the chest of the TU-1 suit is a hose-appendix, through which the diver donned the suit and which he then hermetically sealed by means of a special rubber cord. (From the VIMAIViVS collections)

Fig. 081: Helmet for the TU-1 drysuit. (From the VIMAIViVS collections)

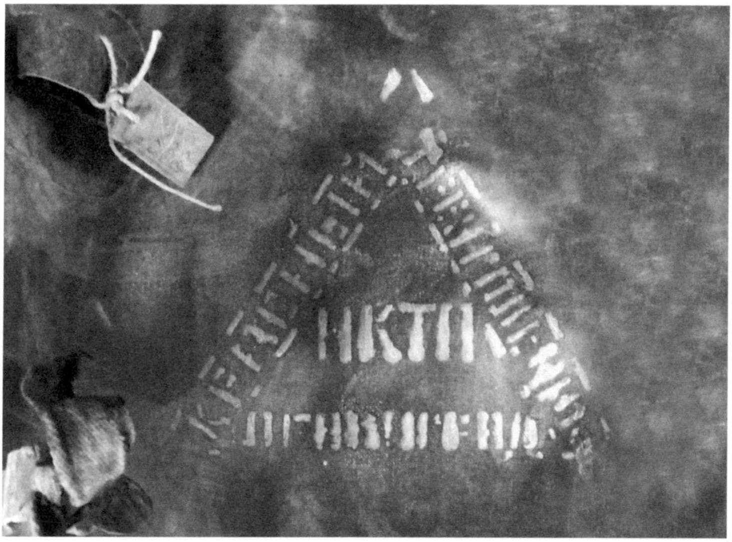

Fig. 082: Stamp of the factory manufacturing the Type E and TU-1 drysuits

The TU-1 drysuit eliminated these deficiencies, to a considerable extent. It had a built-in ShV-3 helmet-mask (Fig. 081), constructed by Dr. Tishkov, a physician and special physiologist, which was fitted with hemispherical ear shells with lobed exhaust valves and special tubular channels that equalized the air pressure to the diver's ears inside the helmet and the water pressure outside the helmet.

The Tishkov helmet, which was suitable enough for the work, had one serious drawback: the pieces of glass in the mask were placed in different planes, at an angle to one another. Because of this, the diver's field of vision was split in two, and it required definite practice to ignore it. Chances are, it didn't matter to Tishkov. Apparently, the pressed molds for gas masks were used to manufacture the diving masks; the relative position of the pieces of glass plays no role in air. But this is inconvenient for a diver under water, and especially disturbing. As it happened, this defect was only corrected after the war, when they began to manufacture masks with glass that was in a single plane.

A second distinction between the TU-1 and the E drysuits, although not an essential one, was the absence of a protective appendix dickey.

The remaining construction of the two suits was similar.

Several examples of the type E and type TU-1 drysuits of prewar manufacture have been preserved up to our time in the VIMAIViVS collections from the Red Triangle Factory (Fig 082).

Lightweight Diving Gear

One more class of diving gear was in existence during the war, which is intermediate between ventilated and light gear, the so-called lightweight diving gear. What is known about it is from the already mentioned *Regulations for the Diving Service*, 1944 edition (Part IV, *Dives in Lightweight Diving Dress (OVS), Harbor Mask and Rigid Diving Dress*) and Volume 2, *Manual for Emergency Rescue and Diving Operations*, published in 1945. This gear was used for inspections and for brief emergency operations at shallow depths.

Two types of lightweight diving gear are known: the domestic OSV and the American type provided on the Lend-Lease program, developed by the Swede, Victor Berg.

OSV gear (Fig. 083) is a TU-1 drysuit with a helmet with an EPRON harbor mask built into the face part, created at the end of the 1920s (its prototype was the Japanese Oogushi mask). It was adopted in the 1930s into the Red Navy's ship equipment.

The operating principle of the OSV harbor mask was extremely unusual. Air was supplied to the diver from the surface by a hose from a manual pump or tanks through a reducer. Inhalation was accomplished when the diver squeezed so-called pincers with his teeth, which consisted of levers on an actuator for opening the air valve. Upon squeezing the levers, the valve opened, and air entered the space below the mask for inhalation. Releasing the pincer levers closed the air valve, and the supply of air ceased. Exhalation was accomplished into the water through a lobed valve built into the body of the mask.

The second type of lightweight, hosed diving gear used during the war was gear developed by Victor Berg and produced by an American firm, the Ohio Rubber Company (Fig. 084).

The equipment consisted, as expressed in modern-day terms, of a full-face mask with built-in multi-stage lung regulator; a medium-pressure, surface-supplied air hose, a set of tanks with high-pressure compressed air, and a pressure reducer or manual air pump.

One feature of this gear is the use of a lung regulator to supply air to the diver.

The operating principle of the lung regulator (Fig. 085) is simple: upon inhaling, a membrane is flexed, it compresses a lever, which is combined with a valve, and allows air into an inhalation chamber and consequently into the diver's mouthpiece. Upon exhaling, the membrane straightens out and the valve closes. The exhaled air exits into the water through the rim of the mask. A distinctive feature of this machine is the double redundancy of the air-supply mechanism: the machine has a pushbutton on the membrane that allows the air supply valve to be forced open by pressing on it (an integral part of all modern lung machines), and a manually rotated bypass relief valve, which opens to pass air from the hose straight into the inhalation chamber.

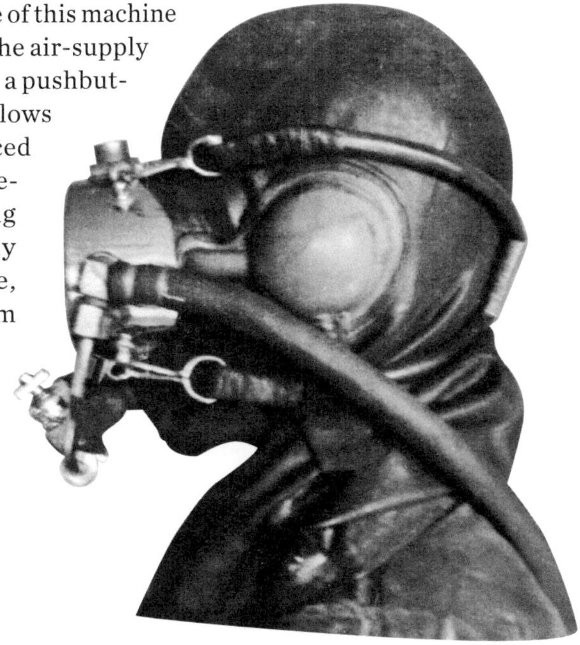

Fig. 083: Lightweight OSV diving gear, consisting of an EPRON harbor mask built into a TU-1 drysuit.

Fig. 084: A full-face mask for lightweight, hosed diving gear from the American firm the Ohio Rubber Company, which was sent to the Soviet Union on the Lend-Lease program during World War II. (Photo from the collection of David Dekker, the Netherlands; www.divinghelmet.nl/www.divescrap.com)

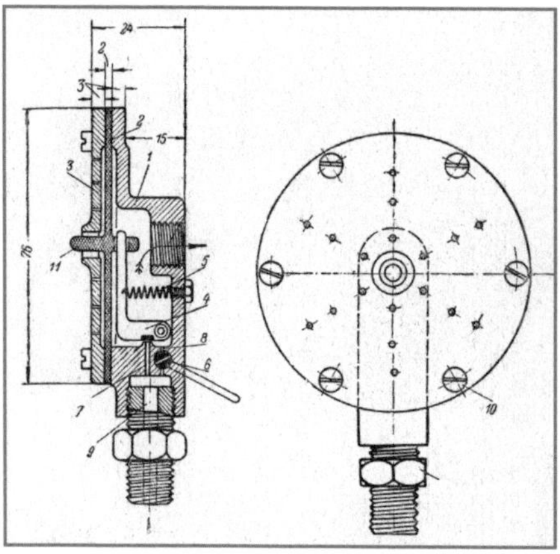

Fig. 085: Technical drawing of a lung machine system for lightweight, hosed diving gear from the American Ohio Rubber Company.

Deep-Water Heliox Gear

The role and place of deep-water dives during the war is not completely understood. Let us point out right away that there are no data on domestic divers making any practical use of heliox gear or a heliox breathing mixture during the war. It is only known that a real possibility existed by that time of undertaking such operations. Before the beginning of the war, in 1937, practice dives were made in the sea at Balaklava to depths of up to 492 feet in a diving bell using a heliox mixture for breathing. In 1940, in the Red Army's barolaboratory at the S.M. Kirov Academy of Military Medicine, a series of experimental dives was conducted in a "hydrobaric chamber," in which the compositions of heliox breathing mixtures and compression and decompression tables were worked out for depths up to 656 feet. Diving gear was also created and tested in practice for these depths, and although it was far from perfect, it was possible to ensure diving, if necessary, to depths of more than a hundred meters and to bring the diver back safely to the surface.

It must be pointed out that the "Regulations for the Diving Service, which were introduced in 1944, did not involve executing deep-water dives. But in the second half of the war, work was started again to introduce deep-water dives into domestic diving practice, which had been interrupted with the start of the war.

At the end of the war, in 1945, a group of our diving specialists and dive physicians was sent to the US, where they went through special training. At the same time, diving specialists from the US Navy were invited to the Soviet Union, and they trained a group of our divers in diving in American heliox equipment.

However, considering our prewar experience in organizing deep-water dives, it may be said that in fact the Americans, who did not disclose to us anything fundamentally new in this area, sped up the actual dives of our deep-water divers under ocean conditions.

In the literature of the wartime period, there is only one mention of heliox equipment that was available to specialists in the navy's emergency rescue service. That is a brief description, photographs, and an operating plan for American deep-water, Mark V Mod 1 (Fig. 86) He-O_2 injector equipment from the Desco company and Buie equipment that is presented in volume 2 of the *Manual for Emergency Rescue and Diving Operations*, already mentioned peviously and published in 1945.

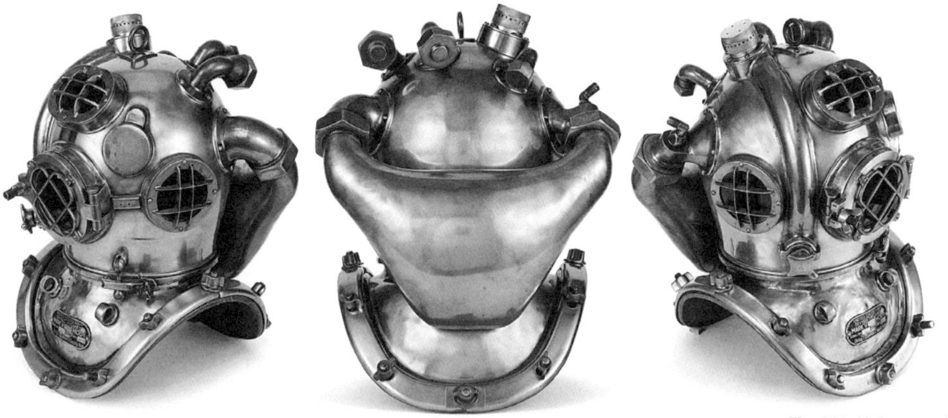

Fig. 086: Helmet and system for regulating a heliox breathing mixture for deep water gear from the US Navy, Mark V Mod 1 HEO2 from the Desko Company. (Photo from the collection of David Dekker, the Netherlands; www.divinghelmet.nl/www.divescrap.com)

By the way, let us say a couple of sentences about a yarn that is widespread in diving circles that the domestic GKS-3M heliox diving gear (Fig. 087) is a copy of American deep-water gear. Without going into detail on the construction, we point out that just a single glance at the helmets for this equipment is sufficient to see how little they have in common.

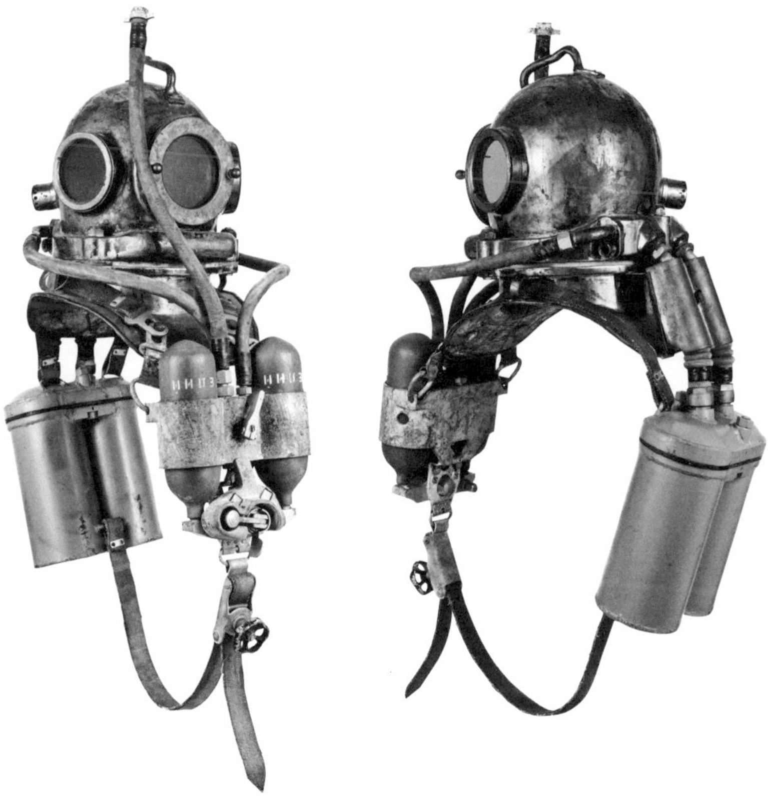

Fig. 087: Helmet and recirculation system for a heliox breathing mixture for GKS-3M deep water gear of the Soviet Navy. (Photo from the collection of David Dekker, the Netherlands; www.divinghelmet.nl/www.divescrap.com)

Sources of Air and Air Distribution

Before the war, two groups of air sources were used for divers in practice: manual dive pumps and motor-driven compressors. It must be supposed that these same ones were also used in the course of the war. In N.I. Fedoseyev and A.F. Maurer's book *Air Management in the Emergency Rescue Service* (Voyenmorizdat, 1946), a very thorough, even exhaustive analysis is presented for compressed air sources used in diving practice from the end of the 1930s to the beginning of the 1940s, and these same items are also the basis of this section.

Motor-driven Compressors

There are also no direct data concerning motor-driven compressors used in the war. It must be assumed that the compressors in fact used are those that were in use in the country's diving elements in the prewar period. It is only known that the first motor-driven air compressors, which began to appear at EPRON diving units at the beginning of the 1930s, were English Heinke and Siebe Gorman, motor-driven compressors (Fig. 088). They were on board EPRON dive boats and rescue vessels, and as of the beginning of the war, on the vessels of the navy's Emergency Rescue Service. Somewhat later, by the end of the 1930s, the production of air compressors for diving was mastered by domestic enterprises, by order of EPRON (Fig. 089).

During the war, a total of seven types of motor-driven air compressors of domestic and foreign manufacture were used on dive boats, with varying efficiency and different operating pressures.

Manual Dive Pumps

Manual air dive pumps were used at mobile dive stations, particularly in the wintertime, on the ice when dive boats could not operate, as well as on board non-specialized vessels (Fig. 090). Basically, two types of air pump were in use: three- and two-cylinder pumps, both imported and of domestic manufacture. It is virtually impossible to determine the type and manufacture of dive pumps from photographs. Their description in the wartime technical literature is of a general nature and does not allow any sort of conclusions to be drawn.

However under wartime conditions, everything was used that could pump air to a diver, irrespective of the date of manufacture. Thus, searchers have been able to find and raise a single-cylinder air pump from a vessel sunk in the Neva during the war, of pre-revolutionary manufacture, judging from the indicator on the pump manometer (Fig. 091).

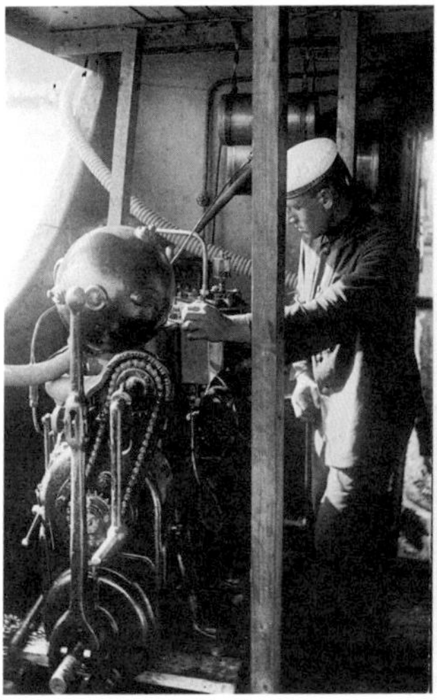

Fig. 088: Motor-driven air pump of English manufacture, Siebe Gorman & Company Ltd., and its installation on an EPRON dive boat. (Photo: middle of the 1930s)

Fig. 089: The first domestic diver's air compressor, created in the middle of the 1930s in accordance with an EPRON technical assignment.

Fig. 090: Manual air pump from the set up operated at a Ladoga dive station. Judging from the absence of a front panel on the pump-box cut out below the manometer and the cast, proprietary manufacturer's label-plate, this was a domestic pump. It is not possible, however, to determine the maker or date of manufacture from this photo. (Photo from the Naval Museum collections, city of Kronstadt)

Fig. 091: Manual, single-cylinder air pump of pre-revolutionary output (on the left), found by searchers on a ship sunk during the war in the River Neva. On the right is the pump manometer dial. (From the archives of A. Mironov)

To supply air to a diver using light equipment, lightweight one- and two-cylinder air pumps of the lever type were used, provided on the Lend-Lease program. Based on the reports of specialists, these pumps were convenient to handle, easy to transport, and quickly put into operation. No photos of lightweight air pumps have been preserved; there is only their technical specification.

A second type of air source for lightweight diving gear was a high-pressure tank with a reducer, which lowered the air pressure to 10–15 atm.

There are no specific data on the practical use of either type of gear for divers in wartime, but their description in the published official handbooks and manuals says, although only indirectly, that they were used.

Air-Regulator Systems

When supplying the diver with air from a manual pump, the diver's air hose was usually attached directly to the pump, and no air-regulator was required.

When operating from dive boats or vessels where high-efficiency, motor-driven compressors were used as an air source and when there was a possibility of two or three divers diving at one time, special air regulation panels were used to distribute the air between the divers (Fig. 092). In principle, the construction of these panels has not changed in decades; their replacement has simply come about due to the appearance of new types of manometers and of shut-off or regulating valves.

Fig. 092: An EPRON three-point air-regulator panel from the end of the 1930s. This type of panel was used on dive boats and rescue vessels throughout the entire war.

 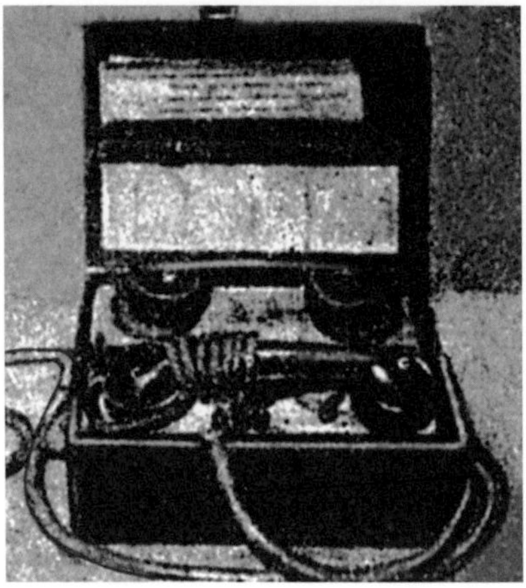

Fig. 093: Telephone post from the Kulakov factory, 1934 (at left).

Fig. 094: GVRU VTS-44 telephone post (at right).

Technical Equipment

The success of a dive is determined not just by the sophistication of the diving equipment, although, without question, this is the most important aspect of a dive. Means of communication and illumination also play an essential role, and in addition, hand tools. What did divers use during the war and what information do we have about such things?

Means of Communication

In 1934, by order of EPRON, industry began to produce the KVL-36 three-conductor, dive telephone post (Fig. 093), which turned out to be extremely successful. The post was intended to provide communications from a ship to two divers at dive depths up to 328 feet. The post had no batteries or signal amplifier. In essence, it was simply a commutator.

The apparent simplicity of dive phone communications (especially at the beginning of the war, there was no thought to amplifying the signal or filtering out noise) was, on the one hand, due to the inability of industry to deliver the number of dive telephone posts needed. On the other hand, it forced the diving services to solve the problem of diver communications independently.

So the forces of the State Military Riverine Administration (GVRU) developed the VTS-44 type, dive telephone post themselves (Fig. 094). It was intended to serve divers in the emergency-rescue, ship-salvage, and hydraulic-engineering services in riverine and lake basins. Judging from the digits in the name, the post was created in 1944.

The main requirement for the new post, created under wartime conditions, was its use of only standard, series-production parts manufactured by our industry. As a result, the post was received in twin wooden boxes fitted with a strap for carrying. It was simple to handle, convenient to use, and did not require highly trained specialists for telephone post maintenance.

In 1943, one of the Moscow factories also made an attempt to create a dive telephone post. The PU-3 piezoelectric diver phone station, with carbon laryngophones, was produced and adopted as equipment. The post was developed without taking past experience into account, and it had a number of essential drawbacks. The laryngophones caused some inconvenience to divers: the carbon powder in them got damp and the laryngophones lost their sensitivity, and the phone fittings, made of ferroelectric material, operated unreliably under marine conditions. The post, as they say, was a "no-go."

There is one other completely puzzling telephone post, the so-called TAG-1. It was produced by a very ambitious enterprise, the USSR Lenin Radio Factory No.197 NKOP, in the city of Gorkiy, which specialized, in addition to other radio electronics products, in various types of voice-acoustic devices, including those for submarines, ships, and aircraft. An incomplete example now on hand came out in 1934 and is preserved in the VIMAIViVS collections (Fig. 095).

A packing box is in the museum, with a small metal plate screwed onto its front side, inscribed "Underwater part for a TAG-1 apparatus," and a plate with the factory name and other data on the side of the box. In the box are a mask-helmet, two telephones and an osteophone, a grounded waist belt, and spare parts (rubber tubes, screw drivers, and other small items).

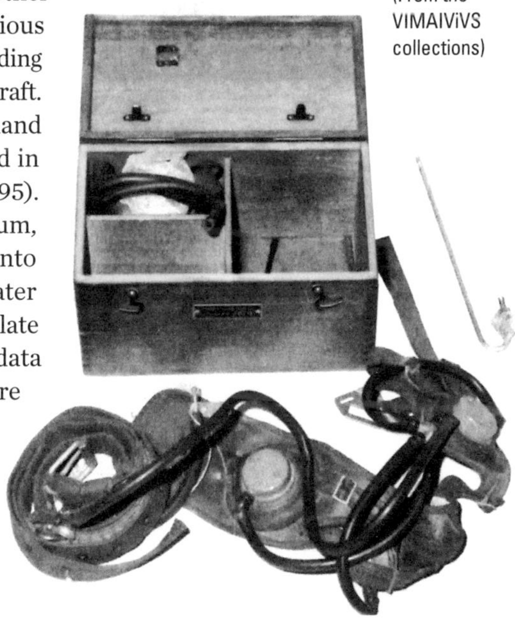

Fig. 095: TAG-1 helmet-mask (at left) and packing box for the underwater portion of the TAG-1 telephone post. (From the VIMAIViVS collections)

Fig. 096: MVTS-3a, three-point telephone post. (From the Naval Museum collections, city of Kronstadt)

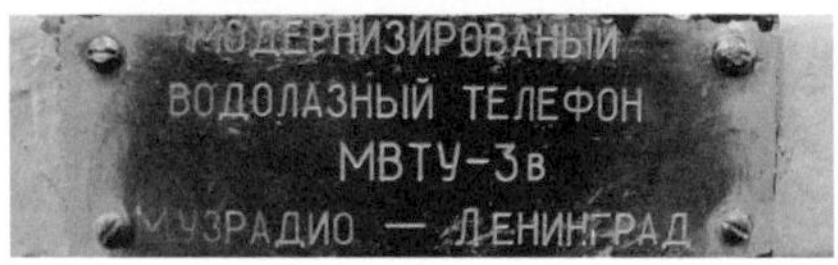

Judging from the mask-helmet with sockets built in for plugging in the phone and microphone fittings and the words "underwater part," which is preserved on its packing box, this is a dive telephone post, notably of factory manufacture. However, it is not known what post this is for, who ordered it, or what its purpose and technical characteristics were. There is no information about it other than the very fact of its existence. In any case, there is no mention, even, of its existence in the literature published by the navy ERS. The post was probably created for use by the Corps of Engineers, and, in complete accordance with the customs of that time, sailors simply knew nothing about it.

And finally, with the completion of the buses for dive telephone posts in wartime, there was the MVTS-3v three-position telephone post from the Leningrad Muzradio Factory (Fig. 096), whose prototype was the American three-position telephone post supplied on Lend-Lease. This telephone post, already robust, had, in addition to commutation of the diver channels, a low-frequency amplifier and a loudspeaker.

Diving Lamps

At the time World War II began, industry had mastered productive capacity and was supplying the diving services with underwater PF-3 and PF-4 lamps (Fig. 097) with cable power from the surface.

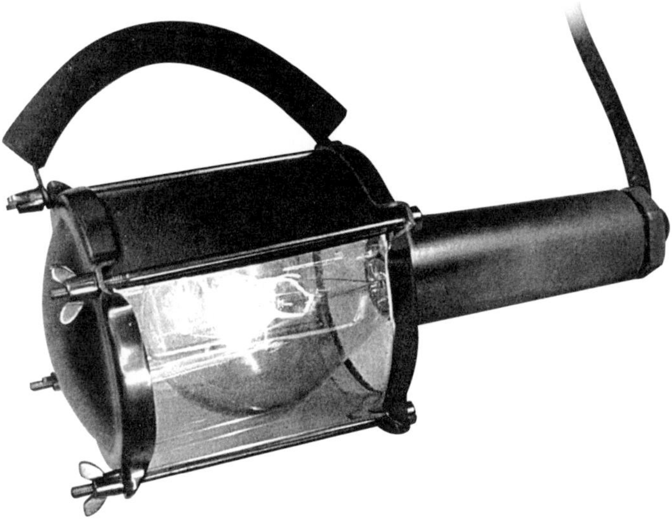

Fig. 097: A PF-4 diver's lamp used in the 1930s. (From the collection of Yu.K. Pavlovskiy, diving specialist)

These lamps had a similar construction and differed from one another in the power used by the bulbs and, as a result, their weight and size. The lamp bulbs operated on 110V and were waterproofed using a glass cylinder pressed into two metal collars.

The PF-3 and PF-4 lanterns were not very convenient to use, and in 1943, the PF-1 and PF-2 underwater dive lanterns that had been developed replaced them. Their principal distinctive feature was that the bulbs for these lanterns operated directly in the water, without a protective glass guard.

The PF-1 lantern for underwater illumination, the Model 1943 (Fig. 098), was intended for general illumination at dive worksites up to 100 m deep. The lantern had a built-in float, which gave it a positive buoyancy allowing the diver to tie it above the work site and leaving his hands free. The lantern's electric bulb, with 1,000W of power at 110V, was silvered inside for the better reflection of light rays, and it shone directly into the water, which cooled it. A sealed cartridge where the electric bulb was screwed in was executed with a rubber sleeve over the body of the bulb and a gasket at the cable inlet.

Electrical power to the lantern was supplied along a 328-foot long cable. The weight of the PF-1 lantern without the cable is about twenty-two pounds.

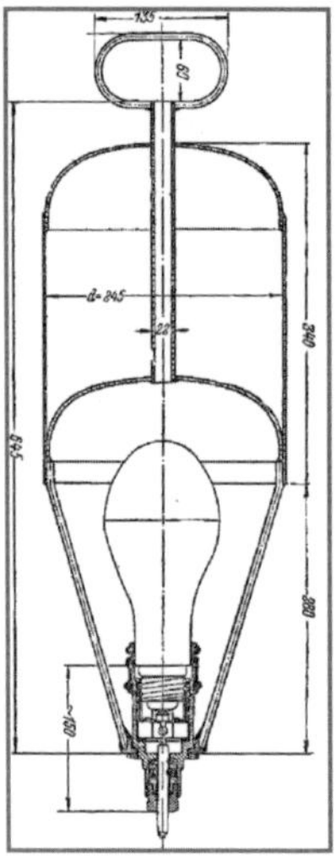

Fig. 098: PF-1 underwater diving lamp for general illumination at operating depths to 328 feet, 1943 manufacture.

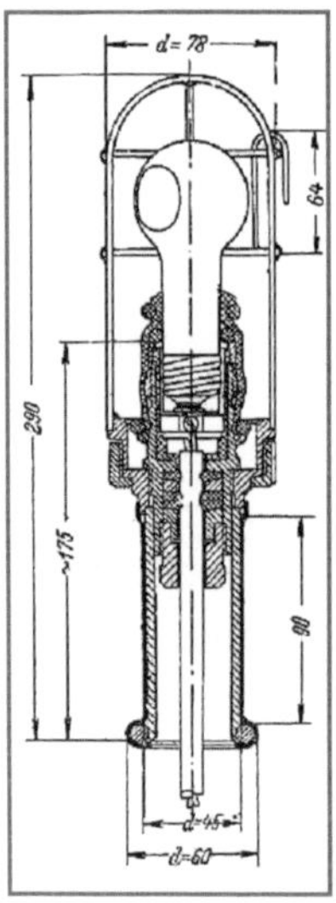

Fig. 099: Portable, manual PF-2 underwater lantern for local illumination, for operating depths down to 492 feet, 1943 manufacture.

The second underwater lantern, the PF-2 (Fig. 099), also developed in 1943, was manual, portable, and intended for local illumination at depths to 492 feet. The lantern's electric bulb, with 150W of power at 100V, also silvered inside, created a light beam directed to the side. A sealed cartridge was executed in the same way as for the PF-1 lamp: by a gasket at the cable inlet and a rubber sleeve on the bulb side. The weight of the light without the cable is 3.5 pounds.

Apart from high-voltage underwater diving lamps with 110V, small low-voltage (12V) manual lanterns were also used in wartime diving practice (Fig. 100). They had a cast metal body with a planar illuminator, in which was disposed a standard, single-filament, 12V automobile bulb. Lantern power was surface-supplied over a cable from a storage battery, which allowed the lantern to be used at a mobile dive station.

Fig. 100: Manual underwater lantern. Supply voltage 12V, lamp output 21W. Power supply was from the surface by cable from a storage battery (from the VIMAIViVS collections). Bottom right, photo: April 1942. Baltic Fleet. (From the RGAKFD collections)

Cutting and Welding Equipment

Cutting and welding metal during the war was done by the electric-arc method using standard electric welding equipment, for the most part, and the specific nature of the diving was hardly considered at all when choosing equipment. For underwater operations, the usual welding generators or transformers were used, with a large-diameter flexible wire and an electrode holder. Very few divers performed underwater electric arc welding, and every underwater welding operation successfully performed, such as installing patches on a hole on the underwater portion of a ship's hull or welding on eyebolts, was particularly noted, and welder-divers were, as we say, few and far between.

Cutting was used more widely than welding. This was arc or oxy-arc cutting, and it was principally used to cut apart the span structures of bridges that had collapsed into the water.

Means of Bottom Scouring

By the beginning of the war, bottom scouring was well developed underwater, using the technology executed in land-based operations. Hardly a single ship salvage, which EPRON divers specialized in before the war, was done scouring underneath the hull of a sunken vessel by means of tunnels in order to stretch a ship-salvage strap in them.

In the war, divers used all types of bottom-processing devices: hydraulic excavators, as well as hydraulic and pneumatic suction dredges. But often none of this was at hand, and then in due course came the usual centrifugal water suction pumps, fire hoses, and fire-hose nozzles, in the role of hydraulic excavators, which operated satisfactorily underwater. And there are certainly no photographs left of working models of bottom-processing devices from wartime, except in specialty literature published in 1945–1946 where there are sketches of them. The most interesting of these were the water-jet ejectors designed by Lt. Col. A.F. Maurer, engineer (Fig. 101).

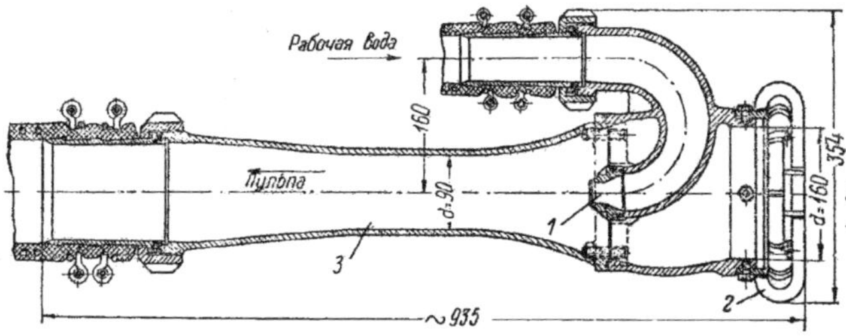

Fig. 101: Technical drawing of a water-jet ejector (suction dredge), designed by Lt. Col. A.F. Maurer, US Corps of Engineers.

In World War II, these water-jet ejectors were in considerable use for underwater engineering operations. In the fall of 1941, vertical ejectors were used in unloading grain and other loose cargo from barges sunk in Lake Ladoga. Based on reference calculations, the efficiency for this type of ejector in operations to scavenge grain was up to 10–12 tons per hour, for a 6-atm head of water.

Subsequently, vertical ejectors coupled with a ZIS-5 hydraulic excavator were used to develop an underwater trench in the River Neva while repairing a siphon on the municipal water-supply line.

One significant operation in which vertical water-jet suction dredges were used as the principal means was the submergence of a pipeline with an inside diameter of four inches and a length of 2.85 running miles, which was laid down on a sandy bottom. In this operation, a trench was developed at a depth of 1.6 feet, with the submergence of the previously laid pipeline and scouring of the bottom to the natural bottom mark.

Divers' Pneumatic Tools

Although direct data have not yet been found on the range of pneumatic hand tools used during the war while performing diving work, judging from the information already mentioned more than once in volume 2, *Manual for Emergency Rescue and Ship Salvage* published in 1945, all types of pneumatic tools were available to divers during the war: chip hammers and pneumatic jackhammers (Fig. 102), pneumatic drills, and boring machines. The principal distinction between the pneumatic tools used for underwater operations and the ones customarily used on land consisted of the former having only one opening instead of several small apertures for expelling exhaust air and with a nipple to which a short rubber hose was connected, with a float made of cork. Air was exhausted into the water via this hose above a diver's helmet, without disturbing his work. When working at great depths, the hose was made longer and was brought to the surface. Power losses were thereby reduced, which were caused by an increase in water pressure at the operating level.

In order to standardize the work of divers using pneumatic tools, the 1939 Unified Standards for Output and Assessment (ENViR) were used for construction work, Section 39 on "Port Hydraulic-Engineering Operations."

An extremely effective means of mechanizing diving operations turned out to be the American Cox system PDP hole-punch and bolt-driver pistol-grip gun, which was supplied to us through Lend-Lease (Fig. 103).

Fig. 102: Pneumatic jackhammer (top).

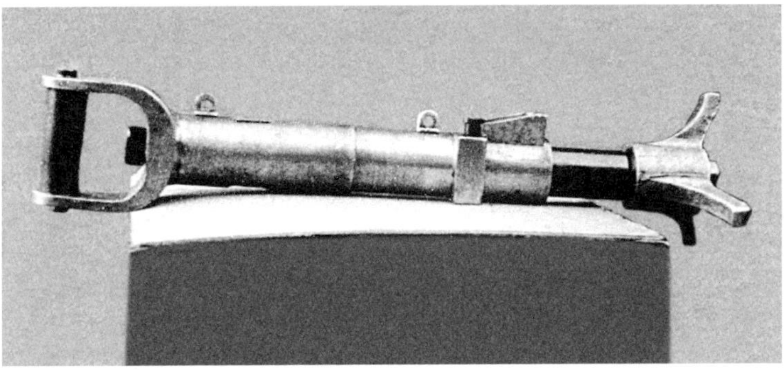

Fig. 103: Underwater hole-punch and bolt-driver pistol-grip gun, Cox PDP system.

The Cox gun replaced, to a considerable extent, such technologically complex and difficult operations as drilling holes in sheet steel. And indeed, using this gun, a diver could drill a hole in a steel sheet up to 0.66-inch thick in one pass or drive a 0.62-inch thread bolt into the sheet. The only serious drawback the gun had was the need to recharge it at the surface.

The gun turned out to be so effective and convenient in operation that in 1943, its production was arranged at Moscow Factory No.3 and handed over to the navy's Emergency Rescue Service.

Weapons

Small Arms

In day-to-day work, divers had no need for small arms. The only exception was for the recon divers of the RON who had to be armed, due to the nature of their combat activity. But neither in the war years nor for a rather long time in the post-war years did there exist a weapon that was especially designed for the use of divers. From the recollections of RON soldiers and scarce photographs (unfortunately

Fig. 104: Carbine, Model 1938.

of very poor quality), it is evident that they used the usual small arms: the Model 1938 carbines, Shpagin PPSh machine pistols, and the Degtyarev DP light machine guns.

The acceptance system adopted in the armed forces of the Soviet Union forced designers to develop a weapon that was not very sensitive, or was completely insensitive, to the effect of heat and cold, sand, dust, dirt, and water, which made its use possible even by recon divers.

The Model 1938 carbine (Fig. 104) was created based on the famous Model 1891/1930 three-line Mosin rifle and differed from the three-line one in its shortened barrel and the absence of a bayonet. The carbine was 3.35 feet long and weighed eight pounds without the shells. The magazine held five rounds, and its effective firing range was 1,100 yards. A 7.62 x 54R cartridge was used in the rifle, and its load was produced by a packet of five rounds each. Though not very comfortable ergonomically, the carbine was quite dependable, technically simple to maintain since it could be broken down without any sort of tool, and on the whole was convenient to use.

Fig. 105: Shpagin machine-gun pistol.

The Shpagin machine pistol (Fig. 105) was adopted into the armament of the Red Army in 1941 and earned full marks from the troops for its dependability and east maintenance. Designed for a 7.62 x 25, Model 1930, pistol round, the machine pistol had a drum magazine for seventy-one cartridges or a box magazine for thirty-five shells, had good action for a distance of up to two hundred meters, and maintained stopping power at distances up to 550 yards. The weight of the machine pistol was twelve pounds with the drum magazine, and 9.5 pounds with the box magazine.

The Degtyarev light machine gun (Fig. 106) was adopted as a weapon in 1927, and it was a very successful product for its time. A 7.62 x 54R cartridge was used in the machine gun, which was placed in a characteristic flat pan, a single-stage magazine that held forty-seven rounds. The machine gun was four-feet long, its weight with a

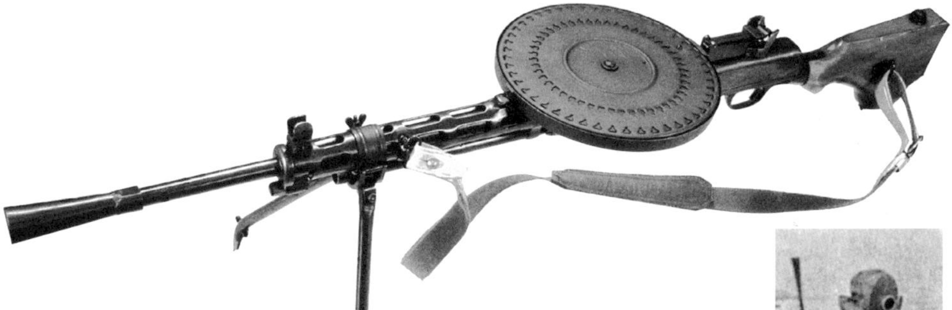

Fig. 106: Hand-held Degtyarev DP-1 machine gun.

loaded magazine was twenty-five pounds, and its effective firing range was up to 1,640 yards. Fig. 106 is a photo of a recon diver armed with the Degtyarev DP-1 light machine gun. In spite of the poor quality of the photo, we can readily identify the machine gun based on the characteristic flash suppressor on the barrel and the round cartridge magazine, part of which is visible below the diver's right hand.

Ammunition, grenade primers, fuses, and other items were sensitive to the effects of water, and RON soldiers carried them in special, sealed rubber bags that they made themselves.

Mines

As it now known, there were no special, high-power mines for divers to use for sabotage purposes during the war, and they had to improvise to blow up the enemy's hydraulic-engineering objects underwater. One of these improvisations was for RON divers to use an anchored naval mine, Model 1908/39, intended for attacking ships with low displacement (Fig. 107). This mine consisted of a spherical military casing with a diameter of 87.5 cm, weighing 604 pounds, armed with 242.5 pounds of explosives, and with an anchor trolley connected to a mine mooring cable. The anchor trolley and mooring cable were in all probability disassembled, so that divers did not to have to pull more than 660 pounds of deadweight metal behind them. Blowing up the mine was done by means of the initiating explosion of a small magnetic mine with a timer, which was attached to the steel casing of the basic mine.

At least two instances are known in which mines were used by Prokhvatilov's combat swimmers: blowing up the bridge across the Narva river at the very beginning of the war and the destruction of the wharf for German boats at Peterhof. An attempt by recon divers

Fig. 107: A naval anchor mine, Model 1908/39, whose spherical military casing was used by RON soldiers to blow up the wharf at Peterhof.

to blow up a bridge in Karelia was not successful, since the water depth at the approaches to the bridge was less than a meter, the bridge guard noticed the divers and opened fire, and the divers had to retreat without accomplishing the mining. It turned out that even while the mine was laid successfully, the explosion still didn't occur, as was later explained, the fuse failed because water had gotten into it.

Still, in one sabotage operation to blow up a bridge across the Dnepr (see chapter 2), diver Viktor Khokhlov simply used boxes of TNT, setting them on the bottom at the bridge pilings.

Nothing is yet known about low-power underwater mines in wartime, aside from the fact that they existed and were used. In any case, they are mentioned as a stand-by means of sapping with a basic charge in all the sabotage executed by divers.

In conclusion, it can be said with confidence that Soviet divers entered the war rather well supplied with both gear and equipment, of course taking into account the day-to-day realities from the end of the 1930s to the beginning of the 1940s. As usually happens, it was not always or everywhere in sufficient supply, especially at the beginning of the war period. Nevertheless, with the problems facing them, the country's diving services managed, both at the front and in the rear.

Conclusion

From a diver's point of view, there were four theaters of military action in the course of the war: the Black Sea, the Baltic, the Barents Sea, and the in-country basins (rivers, lakes, and reservoirs). In each of these regions, divers carried out various operations, but on the whole the problems solved can be grouped in the following way.

Sabotage and reconnaissance operations were executed mainly on the Baltic Sea and to a considerably lesser degree on rivers, virtually on a one-time basis.

Emergency-rescue support for landing operations was provided principally on the Black Sea and to a somewhat lesser extent on the Baltic (including Lake Ladoga and Karelia).

All the remaining types of underwater work, namely rendering assistance to ships in emergencies and the associated ship repair; raising cargo, including weapons and ammunition, from vessels sunk by the enemy, salvaging ships and vessels, mine clearance in the various waters, and hydraulic-engineering work, were carried out in a greater or lesser volume on both seas and inland basins.

What was considered of value in the divers' work, and what did they receive government awards for? An analysis of several hundred award citations presented to divers in all the military theaters has allowed us to make several generalizations.

As a rule, divers were presented awards "for a combination" of a number of specific indicators. Mainly, this was shock work (exceeding norms, multi-hour operations under water, the efficiency of operations performed underwater). This attribute is present in practically all the award citations, with the exclusion of award citations for soldiers in Specops Company, Recon Section, Baltic Fleet Command. There divers were awarded for direct participation in a combat action. Particularly singled out was work under hazardous conditions (under the ice, in strong currents, under sea-swell conditions, in close spaces). An important indicator was dive work under fire or bombardment. The ability of divers to proceed at recognized risk was valued, a risk associated with mine clearance, the salvage of sunken ammunition, the possibility of surfacing without observing decompression procedures, etc. And finally, as usually happened, divers received awards for successfully executing one-time, but vital missions for the command.

The war ended, but its consequences did not disappear.

There remained on the bottom of seas, rivers, and lakes hundreds of thousands of unexploded ammo and thousands of vessels, there were dozens of dams left destroyed and hundreds of bridges, hundreds of underwater pipelines and cable lines needed to be re-laid, dozens of ports had to virtually be built all over again.

In fact, the entire infrastructure in the western portion of the country had to be restored, over which the front lines had rolled twice, leaving behind, both above water and below, broken concrete and torn metal.

And if the main volume of ship-salvage work was done in the first post-war years, even if all the waterways were cleared and practically all the hydraulically engineered structures were restored or rebuilt anew, to this day unexploded shells, bombs, and mines are still being recovered on shore. And they are without number.

In the first post-war years, the country was in desperate need of underwater works, and those years were indeed the "golden century" for diving in Russia: diving elements were created in the ministries that were proliferating in the country, and specialists in the navy together with the shipbuilding, machinery-building, and instrument-making industries did, in fact, re-equip the domestic diving service. Up until very recent times, and in places even to the present day, we use equipment built in the 1950s to 1960s, and not just because nothing else newer was built later, but because in those years, the technology developed was entirely in response to its intended purpose.

The post-war history of diving in Russia includes a lot of unique operations, carried out by divers in the most varied of oceans and at the most varied depths, and they are deserving of their own detailed history.